Call your Mother!

P9-CFJ-643

FOOD &
THOUGHT

RECIPES AND CONVERSATIONS WITH MITCHELL ANDERSON

Food & Thought

Copyright © 2015 by Mitchell Anderson

All rights reserved. No part of this book may be reproduced or transmitted in any form or by any means without written permission of the author.

ISBN 978-0-692-51296-8

DEDICATION

To Richie for cheerleading
To Jenny for teaching
To Rose and Cecile for inspiring
To Mom and Dad for caring

CONTENTS

BREAKFAST

SOUPS

The Light Ones

The Exotic Ones

The Chilled Ones

The Ones for a Whole Meal

SALADS

DINNER TIME

With my mentor Jennifer "Souper Jenny" Levision

SOUPER JENNY

When I think about my life today, I can honestly say, there might not be an Atlanta institution, known as "Souper Jenny", without one of my best friends, Mitchell Anderson. Although, I opened my business four years before Mitchell came on the scene, it was meeting Mitchell and how he became a part of my restaurant family that ended up changing the course of my life forever.

Way back in the early years of Souper Jenny, the fabulous Richie Arpino stopped in one day to introduce me to his partner, Mitchell, visiting from Los Angeles. Mitchell, at the time was a well know LA actor involved in television and film and was thinking about a move to Atlanta to be with Richie and a possible career change. I remember we chatted about his love of food and cooking and It was that day a light bulb went on in my brain and my master plan for Mitchell was hatched!

Shortly before he came into my kitchen that day, I had met with an agency about adopting a child. I was a thirty eight year old entrepreneur and divorced woman and was ready to be a parent! I had only one problem! Who was going to cook while I took off to care for my future newborn? Mitchell!! That's who!

Mitchell came up with an offer that no business owner could refuse. He would work for FREE for three months in our kitchen while I taught him the ropes of how we did things at Souper Jenny and then he would hop in when I was matched with a baby and run things until I could return.

Thus, our love affair began. Mitchell and I would meet each morning at 6:00 AM cook together, laugh together and generally act as silly as possible as we got the shop ready each day. Even years later, when he was in his own kitchen, we would call each other early in the morning trading stories and making each other laugh with our matching personalities and sarcastic wit.

Even early on, Mitchell was a natural in a professional kitchen. He picked up cooking techniques with grace and ease and I quickly saw that we shared the same vision of simple food that was bursting with flavors and color. Mitchell used to make fun of me because I hated using recipes. I would often taste his dishes and comment that they needed more color to match with their flavor. Somehow, he was able to read my mind about what I was looking for. When I left him on his own to create, he always came up with a menu that worked perfectly for the vision of Souper Jenny.

I got the call that I had been matched with a beautiful baby boy being born in Los Angeles on November 6th, 2003. Mitchell didn't even skip a beat when he stepped into his chef role at the restaurant. He was brilliant! It's hard to believe that little baby has grown into my twelve year old son, Jonah.

Mitchell and I worked together almost three years before we both realized that it was time for him to have his own place. It was hard to admit that it was time for him to spread his own wings. I was so proud and impressed that I now had a lifelong friend who shared my passion for the importance of sharing food around the table.

Mitchell always makes sure to give me so much credit when it comes to starting his food career, but words cannot express how much he has given me. I could not have taken the time to realize my dream of becoming a parent without being able to trust the perfect person with my still reasonably new business. We have learned so many lessons together since then.

He may consider me his mentor, but I now truly consider him one of mine.

The recipes and stories in this book are a beautiful life story about one of my favorite people on earth.

I love you, Mitchell!
Jenny

PART 1

Food

Nana and Grandma Circa 1954

FOOD

This is really the story of two grandmothers from two different culinary worlds. Both influenced me in profound ways.

My dad's mother, Cecile Ogren Anderson, was sort of the Webster's Dictionary grandma. A short, sturdy, white-haired woman, she raised six boys and nurtured the world through her kindness and generosity.

And my mom's mother, Rose Francel Rumsey, who, in spite of, or maybe because of, a modest upbringing in Minnesota became quite sophisticated; she had amazing, worldly taste and was a gourmand, before that was even fashionable.

CECILE

"No matter where I serve my guests, it seems they like my kitchen best," read the ceramic plaque above my grandma's wooden trestle kitchen table. I miss that table. I doubt it had much monetary value, but to me, it represented the heart of my family. My generation, my five siblings and I, sat where my dad and his five siblings sat. My grandfather, when he was alive, was, of course, a fixture at one end of the table, The New York Times and Wall Street Journal forever spread in front of him. Often he would be joined by Lloyd, the gardener, Mr. Nelson, the next door neighbor, even John the milkman, taking a break from his daily route.

It sort of didn't matter what time of day it was. Breakfast was early; 7AM at the latest. Eggs, bacon, toast, hot coffee, fresh berries, grapefruit, freshly squeezed orange juice, sometimes French toast or pancakes (always dripping with real maple syrup from the sugar house up the lake). Grandma just kept on cooking until the last one was served. She'd clean up, put the dishes away, and basically start all over again on lunch!

When I was in high school and had access to a car, I'd often bring a half dozen friends out to Bellview (people named their houses back then) to play on the lake. Of course, having a beautiful lake was somewhat of a draw for my friends, but the main attraction was Grandma in her kitchen. This was many years after Grandpa died, so I guess she was happy for the company. There was no crowd too big, no kids too rowdy, and no stomach too empty not to feed and entertain right there at the big table.

Sunday dinners at Grandma's were my favorite. Every other week, my family would pile in the Ford LTD wood paneled station wagon and head up to Bellview, where Grandma was preparing a feast. It wasn't fancy, per se, but it was perfect. More often than not, we'd have a standing rib roast, oven roasted potatoes, some kind of fresh green vegetable, Yorkshire pudding, and an amazing dessert—like Baked Alaska, or "Floating Islands." No matter what she made, it was done with such love, such care, and such ease you never saw her sweat. And no matter how elaborate, how much effort had gone into the preparation of our Sunday feast, she would always say offhandedly, "Oh, it's just catch as catch can."

I guess Grandma's love of food - her deeply held belief that food is what brings people together- inspired me to join her joyful spirit at the stove. It is the warmth of that kitchen, the heart of that amazing house, the sweet aroma of that Sunday roast in the oven that grounds me in my culinary imagination to this day.

ROSE

Nana, as we called her, was quite the opposite. She was tall (at least that's how I remember her), graceful, almost stern—think Kathryn Hepburn in her later years. It's not that she wasn't loving, but her approach to grandmother-hood was simply different than Cecile's. Hers was a more measured, a more ordered world. Having

Grandma and me

Nana on her 90th Birthday

just two children, my mother and my Uncle Buck, there was no doubt more time for the careful consideration of menus, ingredients, tastes, and presentation.

Nana was a voracious reader of cookbooks and cooking magazines. She challenged herself in the kitchen to create culinary experiences, not just meals. If Grandma was Betty Crocker, Nana was Julia Child. Her influences were vast and she appreciated world flavors before it was fashionable.

Meals at Nana and Grampe's house were always served in the formal dining room. The table was set with the finest china, linens, and silver. More often than not, especially in the summertime, all of the vegetables she used to create the meal came from Grampe's garden. I have distinct memories of fresh beets, pulled from the garden, washed with the outside hose and dropped into boiling water. They were cooked al dente in an era where most vegetables were cooked to smithereens. And they were heaven.

My culinary vision, my love of world flavors, my attention to detail in presentation, and yes, my flare for the dramatic (on stage and in the dining room) comes from my memories of Nana. No doubt I'm pulling from sketchy memories from experiences that never happened—you'll have to check with my siblings, but I'm sticking by that story.

I do know that no matter how beautiful the table, no matter how incredible the food, no matter how satisfied the guests, Nana always said something like, "Oh, it needed more salt." Or, "I think it's a little overcooked."

This, of course, was hilarious because it was neither—it was always perfect.

THE COOKBOOK

For many years now, my amazing MetroFreshual Family, my customers, have been asking me for a cookbook. There are a couple of things that make this idea odd. First, I still don't see myself as a real chef. Sure, I've been creating food daily now for about 10 years, and, truth be told, I am my own biggest fan in the kitchen. But deep down, I still feel like an actor who switched stages. I used to be in front of a camera, now I'm in front of a stove. I'm basically a communicator whose medium is food instead of theatre, television and film.

When I apprenticed at Souper Jenny, my mentor and best friend Jennifer Levison taught me an approach to food. She taught me to feel out the whole, not with recipes, but with instinct. True, if she asked me to make a Moroccan Lentil Soup, I had to run to the internet to find out what that meant, but once I got the hang of it, and once I did my homework (which I did on a daily basis) I just let 'er rip and had fun. It was all about creating on the spur of the moment in the Souper Jenny kitchen.

And that's what we've continued to do at MetroFresh for the last decade. It's "Improv Cooking." You're on a stage where the audience throws out four "ingredients" and you create a little scene with the elements they gave you. In the end, you have something that resembles a work of art! Ok, I know that sounds grand, but I'm almost serious. What my chefs and I do on a daily basis is artistic.

Each menu is sort of like a Jackson Pollack painting with lots of color splattered around. It's beautiful in an odd way. And it's odd because we often can't completely figure out how we got there.

We start by prepping raw materials—dicing, blanching, roasting, slicing, cutting, pickling, marinating. And then we just create. We may begin with an idea, a concept, a main ingredient, but by the end wind up in a totally different place. Typically we'll place the salad, soup, dinner entrée, or appetizer in an area of the world and cuisine that inspires us. Maybe it's the distinct flavors of Southeast Asia, or the aromatic spice of India, or the subtle freshness of the Mediterranean. We have the notion, we place the palate, and then we just go. And many decisions along the way are based on color. Nothing sells a salad like vibrant, rich, multicolored fresh ingredients.

Souper Jenny taught me this. I'd be creating some sort of salad for her menu. She'd walk by and offhandedly say, "It needs something red." What did that mean? She'd never tell me, so I just had to figure it out. What she was getting me to understand was that food needs depth and contrast. It's a real thing. I can have eight salads in the case every day. The one with the most contrasting color pallet always sells out first.

The ride is fun and I am fortunate that, literally, hundreds of people get on the boat with us each day. And I can't tell you how many times we've scored big with a certain soup or a particular salad and the customer emails me for the recipe.

Which leads me to the second oddity…

I hardly ever use recipes. Sure, I'll read Gourmet and Bon Apetite, and I have a fairly sizable cookbook library, but mainly I just look at the pictures!

That's actually not true. I do look at ingredient lists. But I rarely follow a recipe. And when I do, it's a chore! I look at the line that says ½ a cup of this and a tablespoon of that, and by the time I pull the measuring cup out of the drawer I've completely forgotten whether it was a ½ a cup or a ¼ of a cup.

So I just make it up as I go along. And, while I've taken the better part of a year to come up with recipes for some favorite MetroFresh dishes, and do hope you'll use them, I hope you'll see them as a gentle guide and not a bible. Be creative. Add or subtract as you see fit. Make your own version—you'll be happy you did and then you can really call it your own.

Breakfast

9

SARAH'S BREAKFAST SPECIAL

INGREDIENTS

2 eggs, fried over easy

Sauteed red onion, bell pepper, Portobello mushrooms, asparagus (Options – zucchini, squash, Brussels sprouts)

Spinach, arugula, kale, or Swiss chard

Avocado for topping

2-3oz. meat protein – Italian turkey sausage, casing removed (other options: sliced steak, chicken breast, bacon, ham, prosciutto, hard salami)

Olive oil

Salt and pepper

Our beloved General Manager, Sarah Peters Kraatz, used to get a special breakfast hand-made by her husband, MetroFresh's Executive Chef Bryan "Rockstar" Kraatz. It always contained a meat protein, a couple of eggs, some kind of sautéed leafy green and usually onions and peppers. Turns out, this was Paleo friendly and we didn't even know it.

As a side note, the Paleo Diet is something of a recent fad. Eating what the cavemen ate, a diet high in protein and natural fats, steering clear of dairy, cultivated grains and processed foods, is supposed to be healthy, give you energy, and make you one with nature.

Our regular breakfast crowd would see Sarah enjoying her own special and began requesting it. So we have "Sarah's Special" on the menu every day. The exact ingredients change, but we keep the Paleo spirit alive for our Paleo friends.

DIRECTIONS

1. Heat 1 TBS olive oil in medium frying pan. Add protein and brown. Add onions, peppers, asparagus, tomatoes. Sautee until vegetables are cooked through but still crispy.

2. In a second frying pan, fry or scramble two eggs the way you like them. Over easy is best; I like the runny yolk.

3. Assemble plate with the green (arugula, spinach or kale) on the bottom. Top that with the sausage sautee, top that with two eggs, and finish it off with a couple slices of avocado! And then, if you're like Sarah herself, pile on the hot sauce. Man, can she eat hot sauce.

SERVINGS

4–6

INGREDIENTS

½ cup yellow or red onions, diced

1 diced and seeded red pepper

1 bunch asparagus trimmed and cut into ½ in pieces

1 ear of corn (in season), cut from the cob

6-8 eggs, well beaten

1 cup shredded gruyere or sharp white cheddar

1 ripe tomato, diced outside flesh

Olive oil

Optional: meat protein, such as Italian sausage, bacon, pancetta, chicken, ham

Sliced avocado

My favorite Sunday brunch at home or at our lake house, when we're entertaining a few friends, is this simple, beautiful frying pan frittata. Pull out this recipe the next time you and your group rents a house in the mountains or heads to the beach. It'll start your Sunday right.

DIRECTIONS

1. Preheat oven to 550 under the broiler. Make sure the rack is closest to the heating element.

2. If you have a cast iron skillet, this is the perfect time to use it. Otherwise, choose a 10-12 inch frying pan, preferably one that doesn't have a plastic handle as the whole skillet will be going under the broiler.

3. Cover bottom of the pan with olive oil and heat on medium high flame until smoking. Toss in onions, pepper, asparagus, and corn and sauté until onions and peppers are tender, but not browning.

4. Note: If you decide you want a meat protein in the frittata, it's best to brown the meat first and then add the vegetables.

5. Pour eggs over the mixture, making sure to cover the bottom of the skillet. Reduce heat to medium and leave egg mixture untouched for about 4 minutes. The bottom of the egg dish will begin to cook through. When you can just see the cooked eggs forming on the side of the pan, add cheese and diced tomato. Salt and pepper to taste and then place in oven under the broiler.

(CONTINUED)

6. It will take about 5 more minutes with the heat from the broiler to cook the frittata through from the top. There should be a nice golden brown crust on the top.

7. Slide a spatula under the eggs and move frittata to a cutting board. Slice into 6 pieces and serve with arugula and a slice of avocado.

NOTE: I do a couple different kinds of frittatas. In the restaurant we do a baked version in the oven, which is great for serving more people. It's also great as an hors d'oeuvre at a cocktail party served at room temp.

You'll use all the same ingredients in slightly greater amounts. Use a greased 9x13 baking pan. You'll have to first roast or sauté the vegetables and just pour the egg over to cover. Sprinkle with grated cheese and tomato and bake for about 45 minutes at 350 or until egg is set and the top is golden brown. Serves 8-10.

CREME BRULE FRENCH TOAST CASSEROLE

SERVINGS

8

INGREDIENTS

1 loaf challah or other spongy white bread, diced into 1 inch cubes

8 large eggs, scrambled

1 cup half and half

1 stick butter

1 cup light brown sugar

Optional – chopped walnuts or pecans

Optional – bananas, blueberries, strawberries, apples, peaches in season

Are you kidding me? There's something called a French Toast Casserole? Whether it's Christmas or Easter, or just a random Sunday, treat yourself to this one! With a big bowl of fresh fruit, some chicken apple sausage (or real down home pork sausage patties) you can't go wrong! It can, and should, be made the day before, put in the fridge, and then cooked off just before serving.

DIRECTIONS

1. Melt butter in a sauce pan over medium heat. Whisk in brown sugar and half and half. Pour mixture on the bottom of a 9x13in. oblong baking pan. It's best to use a spray oil on the bottom and sides of the pan before you put the butter in. If you like, top this with bananas and nuts or sliced strawberries, fresh blueberries, apples or peaches. And for a little crunchiness, sprinkle on some granola!

2. Toss bread cubes evenly to cover the bottom of the pan. Pour in scrambled eggs. Work eggs into the bread with your hands; you want it to soak up the egg. Cover and put in fridge for at least 1 hour or, if you're thinking ahead, overnight.

3. Preheat oven to 350. Bake uncovered for 35-45 minutes. The top of the casserole should be light brown. The center will have the consistency of bread pudding. Pre-cut the slices in the pan. To serve, slide a spatula under each slice and serve with the sticky side up. Top with fresh berries and whipped cream! Decadent, yes, but SOOOO good.

SWEET POTATO HASH WITH TURKEY SAUSAGE, EGGS AND PICO DE GALLO

SERVINGS

6

INGREDIENTS

2 medium peeled sweet potatoes, diced into ¼ inch cubes

½ cup diced red onion

1 red, yellow, or orange pepper diced (for a prettier hash, use peppers of different colors!)

1lb bulk or 4-5 links mild Italian sausage (casings removed)

Fresh thyme leaves

Olive oil

2 eggs per person, served

Pico de gallo (see recipe page 81)

My father loves corned beef hash! It comes out of can and has the consistency, look, and smell of something you might put in a dish for your canine companion. He tops it with a couple of poached eggs and some ketchup and is in heaven. I get that, but it's not for me.

Here's my version, which is marginally healthier and, I think, a lot tastier!

Making the sweet potato hash from scratch does require a little bit of kitchen labor, but like anything, with hard work comes great rewards. Depending on how fast you are with a knife, the initial prep time will be about 10 minutes — not too bad.

DIRECTIONS

1. Heat about 2 tablespoons of olive oil in a large skillet. Add turkey sausage and brown the meat until cooked through. With a slotted spoon, remove sausage while keeping oil in skillet and set it aside. Keeping the pan nice and hot, sauté potatoes, onions, and peppers. If you've diced your potatoes nice and small, it shouldn't take too long for them to cook through and be tender. I like to caramelize the onions and peppers just a bit. When potatoes are cooked through the way you like them, return sausage to the pan. Add a few thyme leaves and salt and pepper to taste.

2. Cook two eggs per person. Over-easy is the most popular, however, sometimes flipping eggs can be difficult, especially if you don't want to break the yolk. I use a non-stick frying pan with a just a touch of olive oil. I'll cook the eggs over medium high heat and cover the frying pan throughout the cooking time. This way, the top of the egg is cooked without having to flip it. Just a little helpful hint!

3. Serve eggs over hash and top them with a little fresh pico de gallo if desired!

Sara Hanna Photography

METROFRESH BREAKFAST BLT

FOR THE JAM

1 pint grape or cherry tomatoes, stems removed and washed

½ cup of raw sugar

2 TBS fresh lemon or orange juice

FOR THE SANDWICH

Two slices multigrain bread (sourdough is good, too!), toasted

Two slices crispy Applewood smoked bacon

2 eggs fried over easy with yolks broken but still just a bit runny

Baby arugula

Tomato jam

When he created "Rockstar" Breakfast at MetroFresh, Bryan (Rockstar) Kraatz would bring me plates of breakfast ideas. My favorite is our take on a traditional bacon, lettuce, and tomato sandwich — the breakfast version with eggs.

The "T" in the BLT for us is tomato jam, which is the only thing in this breakfast deliciousness that will take you a little bit of forward thinking. It's really easy but does require about ½ hour on the stove to cook. You can simply cook down the tomato jam and put it in a sealed container in the fridge. It'll last for a couple weeks.

FOR THE JAM

1. Put tomatoes in a small sauce pan and sprinkle in sugar and juice. Cook over medium low heat, stirring occasionally. The tomatoes will begin to breakdown and the mixture should become almost soupy. Simmer on medium low heat to remove some of the moisture. It will take about 45 minutes. Remove from heat and cool down before transferring to a Tupperware for refrigeration.

FOR THE SANDWICH

2. Assemble sandwich with arugula on the bottom, a little of the tomato jam, bacon, and top with eggs. Serve immediately.

Sara Hanna Photography

METROFRESH SMOKED GOUDA GRITS AND EGGS

SERVINGS

6-8 people

INGREDIENTS

2 cups organic stone ground yellow grits

1 quart half and half

1 quart water

½ stick of butter

Salt to taste – about 1 TBS

1 cup shredded smoked gouda cheese

2 eggs per Serving

Pico de gallo (see recipe page 81)

Grits, you say? How can MetroFresh promote something as delicious and sinful as Smoked Gouda Grits?

Ok, so our philosophy is this. Healthy eating stems from using real ingredients and real food in whatever you're cooking. This dish is not inherently bad for you, but it does pack some calories. So for this dish, think portion size. I think about 8oz or less of cooked grits is plenty. You'll get all the goodness, but still be able to enjoy it without guilt! And your friends, who ventured to your house for brunch, will love you for making them feel comfortable!

DIRECTIONS

1. Bring cream and water to a boil with butter and salt. Slowly whisk in grits and turn heat down to low. Stir occasionally until grits firm up. Turn off heat completely and add cheese.

2. Fry eggs the way you like them. As you may have noticed, I like mine over easy and running all over the place. Place about a half cup of cooked grits into the bottom of a pasta bowl or plate. Top with two eggs and pico de gallo.

A NOTE ABOUT COOKING SOUPS AT HOME

My philosophy is that cooking shouldn't be a chore. Soups require a certain amount of chopping and dicing, so using some items that are pre-cooked, like a rotisserie chicken from the grocery or a good ready-made broth, is not cheating. It's just making your life easier.

For chicken, I buy a whole rotisserie bird, cool it down, and pull off all the meat, discarding bones and skin. Or, if I want to do it myself, I'll buy about eight boneless, skinless chicken thighs, put them in the oven for about 35 minutes at 350, and just dice them into one inch cubes for my chicken soups.

Soups

Vegan, Gluten Free

SERVINGS

Serves 8-10

Yield 3 Quarts

INGREDIENTS

2 cups diced yellow onion

½ cup minced ginger

¼ cup olive oil

2 large butternut squash – about 10 cups, peeled and diced (diced butternut squash is available fresh at Trader Joes – see note about ease!)

3 quarts vegetable stock

1 quart fresh orange juice with pulp

Orange zest and basil chiffonade, for topping

½ cup Vermont maple syrup

Butternut squash is one of nature's wonders. Its naturally creamy, earthy taste can be enjoyed without any guilt whatsoever. We make squash soup all the time — winter and summer, and it's always a best seller. This version is my favorite because of its bright, light ginger/citrus flavor. You'll sweeten it up with a dash of maple syrup, but other than that there is nothing "bad" in it.

DIRECTIONS

1. Heat oil in bottom of eight quart stock pot.

2. Add onions and sauté until translucent.

3. Add butternut squash and enough vegetable stock to cover squash. Bring to a boil. Turn down heat to medium high and continue to cook until squash is very tender.

4. Add orange juice and maple syrup. With an emersion blender, puree soup until smooth.

5. Serve with orange zest and basil chiffonade.

NOTE: Basil chiffonade is just basil cut in fine strips.

Vegan, Gluten Free

SERVINGS

Serves 10-12

Yield 4 Quarts

INGREDIENTS

4 large sweet potatoes peeled and diced

1 15oz can pumpkin or 1 fresh cooking pumpkin, peeled and diced

2 cups diced yellow onion

4 quarts vegetable broth

3 TBS curry powder

½ cup Vermont maple syrup

2 TBS blended canola/olive oil

FOR WALNUTS

1 cup walnut halves

2 TBS olive oil

1 tsp Jamaican jerk seasoning (or cayenne pepper)

2 TBS light brown sugar

1 tsp kosher salt

Much like butternut squash, you can create a sweet potato and/or pumpkin soup using lots of different flavor profiles. This recipe would work for butternut squash as well, with or without the pumpkin. Sweet potatoes and pumpkin are just a little richer in their natural taste, so whatever we add won't be all that powerful.

DIRECTIONS

1. Heat oil over medium high heat in the bottom of eight quart sauce pan.

2. Add onions and sauté for about 4 minutes until they are translucent.

3. Add curry powder and continue to sauté for another minute.

4. Add sweet potatoes (and pumpkin, if using fresh) and then cover with vegetable broth. Bring mixture to a boil and turn down to medium heat, continuing to cook until potatoes are very tender, about 20 minutes.

5. While soup is cooking, toss ingredients for walnuts in a bowl and mix well. Spread evenly on a cookie sheet and bake for about 10 minutes at 350.

6. Add canned pumpkin and maple syrup to soup. Puree in batches in blender or food processor, or if you have one, use a small emersion blender until soup is smooth. Serve immediately topped with sweet spicy walnuts or toasted pumpkin seeds.

LEMON FENNEL ARTICHOKE VEGGIE

Vegan, Gluten Free

SERVINGS

Serves 8-10

Yield 4 Quarts

INGREDIENTS

1 cup diced yellow onion

2 cups diced carrots

2 cups diced celery

1 shredded or finely diced fennel bulb with chopped fronds

2 diced yellow squash

2 diced zucchini

2 8.5oz cans quartered artichoke hearts

4 quarts vegetable broth

½ cup fresh lemon juice

¼ cup blended canola/olive oil

¼ cup chopped fresh dill

While I acknowledge it's not for everyone, I have to say fennel is one of my favorite flavors. With a little lemon, it's just so refreshing in a soup and gives a little pizzaz to an otherwise straightforward vegetable soup.

DIRECTIONS

1. Heat oil over medium/high heat in the bottom of an 8 quart sauce pan.

2. Add onions, celery, carrots, and fennel and sauté for about 5 minutes.

3. Add yellow squash, zucchini, artichoke hearts and vegetable broth. Bring to a boil and turn down to a medium heat. Continue cooking for about 20 minutes or until all the vegetables are tender.

4. Add lemon juice, dill, and serve.

NOTE: This soup will freeze easily, so don't worry about making more than you can eat in a single meal.

SUPER EASY TOMATO BASIL SOUP TOPPED WITH TOASTED PARMESAN CROSTINI

Vegan and Gluten Free (without parmesan crostini)

SERVINGS

Serves 10-12
Yield – 4 Quarts

INGREDIENTS

2 cups diced yellow onion

4-5 cloves chopped garlic

¼ cup olive oil

2 TBS Italian seasoning

4 28oz. cans Cento chef cut tomatoes (or an equivalent quality diced tomato)

2 quarts vegetable stock

1 cup fresh basil

1 baguette

Shaved parmesan cheese

Ok, back to basics. Remember how, on a chilly winter day, mom would make you tomato soup and grilled cheese sandwiches? I know my mom just opened up a can of Campbell's soup, added some water (or more often than not, some whole milk), and called it a day. Of course, we'll get a little more creative with our ingredients, but there's hardly any chopping or dicing. You'll want to get an emersion blender to make your life easier, but other than that, this is soup simplicity 101. Topped with a toasted parmesan crostini and you have your cheesy soupy combo all in one.

DIRECTIONS

1. Heat oil on the bottom of an eight quart stock pot.

2. Add onions and garlic and sauté until onions are translucent.

3. Add Italian seasoning and sauté for another minute. Add tomatoes and vegetable stock and bring to a boil. Turn down to medium heat and cook for another 30 minutes.

4. Add basil and, using your emersion blender, puree soup until smooth.

FOR THE PARMESAN CROSTINI

Prepare while soup is simmering on stove.

1. Lay 12 or more slices of baguette on a cookie sheet. Drizzle with good extra virgin olive oil. Sprinkle with salt, pepper, and Italian seasoning and put in preheated 350 degree oven for about 7 minutes.

2. Place a small amount of shaved parmesan on each toast piece and return to the oven for another 3-4 minutes until they are golden brown. Serve soup in bowl topped with crostini.

ALTERNATIVES: Add 2 cups diced day-old bread or croutons and 1 cup diced fresh mozzarella for a delicious Italian tomato bread soup.

OR: Add 1 cup crumbled goat cheese before blending the soup.

OR: Serve this soup cold in the summertime topped with green onion and crème fraiche.

Vegan and Gluten Free
(without Crouton and
Butterscotch)

SERVINGS

Serves 8-10

Yield – 4 Quarts

INGREDIENTS

Two large butternut
squash, about 8 cups,
peeled, seeded, and diced
into two inch squares.

1 diced yellow onion

3 peeled and diced Granny
Smith apples

2 TBS blended
canola/olive oil

3 quarts organic
vegetable stock

2 cups fresh apple cider

½ cup brown sugar

Butterscotch
topping – preferably in a
squeeze bottle

Half stick of butter

1-2 cloves minced garlic

1 baguette

As you probably surmised, I do love my butternut squash! We've done it with ginger and orange, and now we're going to accent it with apple, brown sugar, and a little butterscotch. I originally created this recipe for a dinner we had featuring a very fancy chardonnay with butterscotch and apple in its flavor profile. It was a big hit. For a starter, in which your main course is some sort of rich braised meat, this particular squash soup is the perfect light, zingy intro!

DIRECTIONS

1. Heat oil in the bottom of an eight quart stock pot.

2. Add onion and apples and sauté until onion is translucent.

3. Add butternut squash and just enough vegetable broth to barely cover. Bring to a boil and cook for about 20 minutes until squash is very tender – so it breaks apart with a fork.

4. Toast crostini while soup is cooking. Melt butter in a small sauce pan. Add minced garlic and whisk around. Drizzle onto thinly sliced baguette on a cookie sheet. Bake in oven at 350 for about 10 minutes until crispy.

5. Add apple cider and brown sugar to the soup. Puree with emersion blender (or in batches in a food processor) until smooth.

6. Serve in small coffee cups or small soup bowl topped with crostini and a "crisscross" drizzle of butterscotch sauce.

"CREAMY" CREAM-LESS ASPARAGUS SOUP TOPPED WITH CRISPY LEEKS

Vegan, Gluten Free

SERVINGS

Serves 8-10

Yield 4 Quarts

INGREDIENTS

1 diced yellow onion

2 cups diced celery

5 cups peeled and chopped asparagus, about 5 bunches (peeling the asparagus is not essential but it will make a better soup)

4 quarts vegetable stock

1 ½ cups white rice

¼ cup olive oil

1 cup white wine

1 TBS chopped fresh tarragon

2 sliced leeks (Use only the bottom, white part of the leek and slice thin)

1 cup canola oil

Ok, so I know people sometimes think asparagus soup is a little too strong. I happen to love it, so I'm including it in the book. This version uses some white rice as a thickening agent rather than a traditional roux and cream, which makes the soup gluten free and vegan.

DIRECTIONS

1. Heat olive oil in the bottom of an eight quart sauce pan.

2. Add onions and celery and sauté for about 4 minutes.

3. Add asparagus and vegetable stock and bring to a boil. Turn heat to medium and cook for about 30 minutes until celery and asparagus are very tender.

4. Add rice and cook for another 30 minutes. You want the rice to almost dissolve in the soup. Puree with emersion blender or in batches in the food processor until smooth. Return to heat and serve topped with crispy leeks.

FOR CRISPY LEEKS

1. Heat oil in a small sauce pan over high heat.

2. You can check to see if oil is hot enough by dropping in one shaved leek piece. If the oil bubbles, then you're ready. Sprinkle the leeks in the oil slowly. **Dropping anything into hot oil is living dangerously because the moisture in the leeks will escape immediately – use caution.**

3. Stir occasionally with slotted spoon. As leeks begin to brown, remove from oil with the spoon and place on paper towel to absorb the oil.

4. Top with a little kosher salt.

5. Serve soup in bowls topped with crispy leeks.

THAI COCONUT CHICKEN

Gluten Free

SERVINGS

Serves 10-12

Yield – about 5 Quarts

INGREDIENTS

1 cup diced yellow onions

2 cups diced carrots

2 cups diced celery

¼ cup blended olive/canola oil

½ cup minced fresh ginger (use a food processor)

4 quarts chicken stock

1 cup Thai sweet chili sauce

1 pint white button mushrooms, cut in half

2 12oz can lite coconut milk

Meat from one 3-4lb cooked whole chicken, pulled from bone, or 8 chicken thighs

1 cup uncooked rice

2 cups chopped cilantro

The best thing about serving lots of soup at MetroFresh is that we can travel the globe. This soup, inspired by Thai flavors, is the right mix of spicy and sweet. I happen to love Thai sweet chili sauce and consider it the secret ingredient in many MetroFresh dishes.

DIRECTIONS

1. Heat oil in the bottom of an eight quart stock pot.

2. Add onions, carrots, celery and ginger and sauté for about 4 minutes until onions are translucent.

3. Add mushrooms and continue to sauté for another 3 minutes.

4. Add chicken stock and sweet chili sauce and bring to a boil. Turn down to medium and continue to cook for about 30 minutes.

5. Add chicken and turn heat to medium low and continue to cook for another 30 minutes.

6. Add rice and continue to cook until rice is tender.

7. Finish with coconut milk and fresh herbs. Serve immediately.

SPICY NORTH AFRICAN CARROT AND PEANUT SOUP

Vegan and Gluten Free

SERVINGS

Serves 8-10

Yield – about 4 Quarts

INGREDIENTS

2 cups diced yellow onions

8 cups diced carrots

1 cup diced celery

2 TBS minced ginger

2 TBS minced garlic

¼ cup blended olive/ canola oil

2 TBS Chinese chili and garlic sauce (more or less depending on how spicy you want your soup to be)

1 TBS ground cumin

1 TBS curry powder

3 sweet potatoes peeled and diced

5 quarts vegetable stock (chicken stock can also be used)

1 cup creamy peanut butter

½ cup lime juice

Chopped peanuts and cilantro for topping

Every day in the MetroFresh kitchen, we try to take our customers on a journey. In the wintertime, when six huge pots of soup are boiling on the stove, the aromas of countries from several continents fill the air. From North Africa, we take ginger, spicy chili paste, a little cumin, and peanut butter to create this most exotic of the exotic soups. Frankly, it's not for everyone, but I happen to LOVE it.

TIP: Easy way: Mince garlic and ginger together in food processor.

TIP: Butternut squash or pumpkin can be used instead of sweet potatoes.

DIRECTIONS

1. Heat olive oil in the bottom of an eight quart stock pot.

2. Add in onions, celery, ginger, and garlic and sauté until onions are translucent.

3. Stir in all dry spices and chili paste and sauté for another 4 minutes.

4. Add carrots, sweet potato, and vegetable stock and bring to a boil. Turn heat down to medium and continue to cook for about an hour or until carrots and sweet potatoes are very tender.

5. Add peanut butter and lime juice. If you have an emersion blender, this is the time to use it. You will puree the soup right in the pot. Or, use a food processor and puree soup in small batches, returning each batch to another soup pot.

6. If soup is too thick, you can always add a little more vegetable stock or water.

7. Serve soup topped with cilantro and chopped peanuts.

Gluten Free

SERVINGS

Serves 10-12
Yield 4 Quarts

INGREDIENTS

1 cup diced red onion

2 cups diced carrots

2 cups diced celery

2 TBS minced garlic

2lbs pork shoulder with
fat trimmed and cut into 2
inch pieces

¼ cup olive oil

2 TBS ground cumin

2 TBS ground ginger

2 TBS Jamaican jerk spice

1-2 Tsp cayenne pepper
(optional)

4 cups dried black beans
(soaked overnight
if possible)

6 quarts vegetable stock

2 cups fresh diced
pineapple (1 inch chunks)

Sour cream and chopped
green onions (optional)

Rockstar's wife and MetroFresh's General Manager, the adorable Sarah Kraatz, absolutely LOVES this soup. She asks for it practically every day. If it's on the menu and she's serving soups that day, chances are she'll steer you to it. You can make this soup without the pork for vegetarian variety, and, if you think adding the pineapple is too weird, you can leave it out, but I think that little sweet surprise of pineapple really gives this basic soup that tropical flair. You'll be saying "Yah, Man," all day, brother. Welcome to Jamaica and have a nice day!!

DIRECTIONS

1. Heat oil in the bottom of an eight quart stock pot.

2. Add in diced pork and brown on all sides.

3. Add onion and garlic and continue to sauté until onions are translucent.

4. Add celery and carrots and dried spices. Sauté for 4-5 minutes more.

5. Add soaked black beans and vegetable stock and bring to a boil. Turn heat down to medium and cook for about two hours or until black beans are very tender. Stir often so beans don't stick to the bottom of the pan.

6. If you'd like a thicker soup, use an emersion blender and blend just a bit. You can pulse the blender to just break apart a few of the black beans.

7. Add pineapple and serve. Top with sour cream and green onions if desired.

RED CURRY COCONUT SPLIT PEA

Vegan and Gluten Free

SERVINGS

Serves 8-10

Yield 3 Quarts

INGREDIENTS

1 cup diced yellow onion

2 cups diced carrots

2 cups diced celery

2 TBS minced ginger

2 TBS minced garlic (Easy way – mince garlic and ginger together in food processor)

¼ cup blended olive/canola oil

2 TBS red curry paste

4 cups Yellow (or green) split peas

4 quarts vegetable stock

1 13oz. can coconut milk

Split Pea Soup is another MetroFresh favorite. We make it so many different ways, choosing one is nearly impossible. I've decided to give you the "exotic" version since it's just that much different and basically, that's the MetroFresh way!

DIRECTIONS

1. Heat oil in the bottom of an eight quart stock pot.

2. Add onions, carrots, celery, garlic and ginger and sauté for about 4 minutes until onions are translucent.

3. Add curry paste and sauté for another two minutes.

4. Add dried split peas and stir into mixture for a minute to "toast" the peas.

5. Add vegetable stock and bring to a boil. Turn soup down to medium low and continue to cook for about an hour. Be sure to stir this soup while it's cooking; as the peas break down, you don't want them to burn or stick to the bottom of the pan.

6. The soup is ready to serve when the split peas have broken down and the soup has become thick. Just before serving, stir in coconut milk. If soup is too thick for you, add a little water and stir.

Gluten Free

SERVINGS

Serves 8-10
Yield – 4 quarts

INGREDIENTS

1 large diced yellow onion

2 cups diced carrots

2 cups celery diced

3-4 minced garlic cloves

¼ cup blended olive/
canola oil

1 TBS each of
ground turmeric,
cumin, cinnamon

½ Tsp ground clove

1 cup golden raisins

½ cup chopped
dried apricots

4 quarts chicken stock

Meat from one 3-4lb
cooked whole chicken or 8
chicken thighs

2 cups uncooked
Moroccan couscous

Now we go to Morocco, where aromatic spices abound. With a rich combination of spices and Moroccan couscous, this soup is almost like an exotic chicken porridge. You may choose to leave the couscous out of the soup itself, ladling the soup over some cooked couscous instead.

DIRECTIONS

1. Heat oil in the bottom of an eight quart stock pot – medium high heat.

2. Sauté onions, garlic, carrots, and celery until onions are translucent.

3. Add dry spices and sauté for another 3 minutes.

4. Add chicken stock and bring to a boil. Turn heat down to medium and cook for another 30 minutes. Add chicken, apricots and raisins. Cook for an hour.

5. Add dried couscous and turn heat off.

6. Serve after about 5 minutes, when couscous is tender.

GAZPACHOS! OLE!

Vegan and Gluten Free

SERVINGS

Serves 4-6

Yield – 2 quarts

THE BASICS

1 red pepper –
seeded and diced

1 green pepper –
seeded and diced

½ cup diced red onion

¼ cup chopped cilantro
(more or less to taste)

2 TBS hot sauce (more or
less depending on taste)

Kosher salt to taste

FOR THE TRADITIONALIST

1 peeled, seeded, and
diced hothouse cucumber

2 cloves chopped garlic

4-5 vine ripe
tomatoes –
seeded and diced

1 cup ice

1 cup water

There's nothing like a refreshing cold soup on a hot summer day. Gazpachos of all kinds are super easy and, as a bonus, almost calorie free! For our purposes, we're going to start with the basic ingredients: peppers, red onions, cilantro, and hot sauce. Then I'll give you alternatives to make them that much better! For traditional tomato gazpacho, you'll use cucumber and tomato. But I'm going to throw out some other ideas that you can experiment with, omitting those two ingredients.

DIRECTIONS

1. Basically – put all the ingredients into a food processor and blend on pulse until the soup is the consistency of a loose salsa. You'll probably have to do it in batches and mix at the end in a bowl. Chill for an hour or so. This soup will keep in the refrigerator for two or three days.

ALTERNATIVES:

FOR A LITTLE TROPICAL FLAVOR: ½ diced fresh pineapple (instead of the cucumber and tomato)

WHEN PEACHES ARE IN SEASON AND DELICIOUS: About 6 peeled and diced peaches

LATE SUMMER FLAVOR: 1 diced watermelon (you don't have to add water to this one)

FOR A "WHITE" GAZPACHO: 4 cups seedless white grapes, ½ cup slivered almonds or walnuts and 1 cup celery

Vegan and Gluten Free

SERVINGS

Serves 6-8

Yield 2 Quarts

INGREDIENTS

2 peeled and diced hot house or European cucumber (If you're growing cucumbers in your garden, they are probably the conventional variety, in which case you'll need to peel and seed them.)

1 peeled, seeded, diced cantaloupe

¼ cup diced red onion

1 cup fresh orange juice

½ cup fresh basil

A few ice cubes

Kosher salt to taste

When I lived in New York City the summer I graduated from college (back in the dark ages) I lived on cantaloupe and cottage cheese. I know, it was a little like grandma at the corner diner getting her "diet" plate. But here's the thing: a fresh, ripe cantaloupe, when it's ready to eat, just tastes like summer. The combination of cucumber and cantaloupe, with savory basil, makes this soup such a refreshing, light summer starter.

DIRECTIONS

1. Use your food processor or juicer. Blend the onion and basil first. Then add cucumber, cantaloupe, basil, orange juice, and ice. Blend until smooth. Serve immediately or store in container in refrigerator. The soup will separate slightly after sitting, so before serving be sure to stir it.

SERVINGS

Serves 4-6

Yield – 2 quarts

INGREDIENTS

4 cups peeled, diced fresh mango, or 4 cups mango nectar or puree

1 15oz. can coconut milk

1 32oz. container plain non-fat or lo-fat yogurt

¼ cup organic honey

Toasted coconut for topping

Ah, for a taste of the tropics. While not very "lo-cal" this soup is just a little exotic; that is, if you don't happen to be living in Kawaii. It's just a little sweet, and some people at the restaurant save it for dessert. It's almost like a smoothie and can be made either with fresh mango, mango nectar, or mango puree.

DIRECTIONS

1. Puree fresh mango in food processor, add coconut milk and yogurt. Blend until smooth. Add honey until it's just sweet enough for you.

NOTE: If you use fresh mango or mango puree, you'll most likely have to add a little more honey. If you're using mango nectar, it may be sweet enough without the honey.

2. Toast a small amount of shredded coconut on a sheet pan until just golden. At 350, it'll take less than 10 minutes.

3. Serve in a bowl with a little coconut on top and a mint leaf for color.

This chilled cucumber soup with dill and yogurt is a little like diving into a cool lake and swimming 50 yards. It kind of wakes you up and makes you feel better at the same time.

SERVINGS

Serves 4-6

Yield – 2 Quarts

INGREDIENTS

2 peeled "hot house" or European cucumbers or 4 conventional cucumbers, peeled and seeded

¼ cup diced red onion (more or less to taste)

1 32oz. container lo-fat or non-fat yogurt

2 TBS chopped dill

2 TBS fresh lemon juice

Kosher salt and pepper to taste

DIRECTIONS

1. Use your food processor to blend the ingredients in this order – onion, cucumber, dill, yogurt, and lemon.

2. Serve in a small cup with a very thin slice of lemon and sprinkle chopped dill on top.

Vegan – Gluten Free

SERVINGS

Serves 6-8
Yield - 3 Quarts

INGREDIENTS

1 whole medium
seedless watermelon,
rinds removed and cut
into cubes

2 peeled and diced
seedless hothouse
cucumbers or 3-4
peeled, seeded and diced
green cucumbers

½ cup chopped
green onions

2 TBS peeled,
chopped ginger

2 TBS chopped Thai basil

1 TBS chopped cilantro

1 TBS Sriracha chili sauce

Kosher salt to taste

Years ago, when I was in Thailand (doesn't that sound exciting?) I was so impressed by the distinct flavors of the food. Every ingredient was present in the mouth. This chilled soup is thin, to be sure, and won't fill you up, which is a plus during the summer, but for a delicate taste with lots of interesting flavors, you can't beat it. Serve it for a light summer lunch or brunch and your guests will be thrilled.

Chill all the ingredients before using. You're not going to want to add ice to this one — it's already thin enough.

DIRECTIONS

1. There are two ways to prepare this soup, depending on your equipment. If you have both a food processor AND an emersion blender, get 'em both ready!

2. First, in the food processor blend ginger, then add cucumber. Finally, add green onions and blend until smooth.

3. If you're using an emersion blender, place diced watermelon in a deep bowl then add the blended ingredients. Or, working in batches with a food processor, add watermelon and blend. You'll stir in everything in the end, so don't worry about doing a little at a time and transferring to a serving bowl. Add Thai basil, cilantro, and Sriracha and blend once more. Finally, salt to taste.

NOTE: Thai Basil is hard to find. You most likely will have to go to a good farmers market or Asian specialty store. If you can't find it, you can try using regular basil, or just omit it altogether.

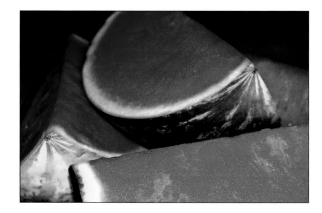

IRISH LAMB AND POTATO STEW WITH GUINNESS

SERVINGS

Serves 8-10

Yield – about 4 quarts

INGREDIENTS

3lbs. lamb stew meat, diced

5 medium size Yukon Gold potatoes, diced into 8 large pieces

1 cup diced yellow onion

2 cups diced celery

2 cups diced carrots

4 stems fresh rosemary

4 stems fresh thyme

3 quarts beef or lamb stock (use vegetable stock if you can't get a good beef stock)

1 18oz can Guinness Ale

¼ cup olive oil

Salt and pepper to taste.

My idea of the perfect winter dinner is a big bowl of lamb stew, a tossed green salad, and a crispy baguette. Serve this rich, bold lamb stew in front of a roaring fire and you'll feel like you've been transported to nineteenth century Dublin.

DIRECTIONS

1. Heat oil in the bottom of a 10 quart stock pot over medium high heat for about 2-3 minutes. Toss in lamb and brown on all sides. Then add onions, celery, carrots and sauté for 4-5 minutes longer. Add Guinness. Bring to a boil and reduce by 1/3. Add in potatoes and stock and return to a boil. Immediately lower heat to a very low simmer. Toss in 4 stems each rosemary and thyme; you can fish out the stems later. Cook stew for minimum of two hours until meat is very tender. The longer you cook it, the better it will be.

2. The whole affair can be done in a crock pot and cooked all day. You'd most likely have to adjust quantities for a crock pot, but cooking it all day is just the ticket for a really delicious rich lamb stew.

3. Serve in large soup or pasta bowl with a sprig of rosemary for garnish, some toasted baguette or ciabatta and Irish butter.

Sara Hanna Photography

MITCHILI (MITCHELL'S TURKEY CHILI)

Gluten Free

SERVINGS

Serves 10-12

Yield – About 5 Quarts

INGREDIENTS

2lbs. ground turkey

1lb. (about five links) hot Italian turkey sausage, casings removed

1 large red onion, diced

1 each red, yellow, green pepper, seeded and diced

3 28oz. cans chopped tomatoes

1 16oz can each of chili beans, great northern white beans, kidney beans and black beans (drain all except for chili beans)

¼ cup olive oil

¼ cup chili powder

2 TBS ground cumin

2 TBS ground coriander

½ cup Dijon mustard

¼ cup chopped fresh dill

1/2 bunch chopped cilantro

Kosher salt to taste

Shredded cheddar cheese

Sour cream

The name Mitchili came from my days at Souper Jenny. There was a crazy, hilarious server there with Lucille Ball flaming red hair named Meredith, who every time I walked through the door would shout, "Mitchili!" So when I opened MetroFresh, naturally my chili had to be called "Mitchili."

(Please pronounce it as one word — it's Mitchili, not Mitch — chili!)

I make Mitchili at MetroFresh every day of the week. This recipe will easily serve 10-12 people. With a salad and some warm French bread, it's the perfect crowd pleaser at your Super Bowl Party when the weather is cold, and with grilled hot dogs and slaw it makes a perfect summer backyard BBQ. I am also giving you the home version which uses hot Italian turkey sausage so it will be a little spicier than the MetroFresh version. I suggest doing what I do: look at the recipe and use it as a jumping off point. Be creative. Mitchili is really just a state of mind!

DIRECTIONS

1. In large stock pot heat olive oil and then toss in onions and peppers. Sauté until just tender, about five minutes over medium heat. Do not allow them to brown.

2. Add turkey meat and sausage and sauté until cooked through.

3. Add dry spices and mustard. Continue to cook meat until it has turned the color of the chili powder.

4. Add tomatoes and simmer for about 10 minutes.

5. Add beans and cook over low heat for about an hour. Stir every once and a while so the beans don't burn to the bottom of the pot.

6. Add fresh herbs before serving and salt and pepper to taste. Serve with sour cream and cheddar cheese if desired.

7. I serve it over white or yellow rice for an even heartier meal.

CHICKEN POT PIE SOUP TOPPED WITH PUFF PASTRY

SERVINGS

Serves 12-14

Yield – About 6 Quarts

INGREDIENTS

1 cup diced yellow onion

2 cups carrots halved along the length and sliced into half moons

2 cups diced celery

¼ cup blended canola/olive oil

4 medium size Yukon Gold potatoes, diced into 2-inch cubes

2 cups frozen peas

2 cups frozen corn

1 jar pearl onions (or 1 bag fresh peeled pearl onions)

1 cup cooking sherry

3 sprigs each of rosemary, sage, and thyme tied with butcher's twine (this is called a bouquet garni)

4 cups pulled chicken meat or diced thigh meat

3 quarts chicken stock

1 quart whole milk (can be omitted if you wish it to be dairy free)

1 package frozen puff pastry sheets

This is one of my favorite "whole meal" soups. Whenever I make it at the restaurant it sells out. During the long, cold winter a taste of comfort is what you need.

DIRECTIONS

1. Heat oil in the bottom of a 10 quart stock pot.

2. Sauté onions, carrots, and celery until onions are translucent.

3. Add in cooking sherry and sauté for another 2-3 minutes. Add in potatoes, corn, peas, and pearl onions. Cover with chicken stock, toss in bouquet garni, and bring to a boil. Turn heat to a slow simmer and continue to cook for about 30 minutes or until vegetables are tender.

4. Add in cooked chicken pieces and cook for an additional 15 minutes.

5. Add milk and serve immediately in large bowls topped with puff pastry.

FOR THE PUFF PASTRY: Follow directions on the box. For ease of serving, after dough thaws, cut into 4 inch squares before baking.

NOTE: Soups with potatoes do not freeze very well, so this might be a good time to invite friends, or take a gift of soup to the neighbors.

BEEF LASAGNA SOUP

SERVINGS

Serves 12-14

Yield – about 6 Quarts

INGREDIENTS

1lb ground beef (or ground turkey if you want to be lean)

¼ cup olive oil

1 cup diced yellow onion

2 cups diced celery

2 cups diced carrots

5-6 cloves minced fresh garlic

3 TBS dry Italian seasoning

1 cup red wine (optional)

2 28oz. cans diced tomato

4 quarts vegetable stock

1 15oz. container ricotta cheese

1lb. shredded mozzarella cheese

1 cup shaved parmesan

3/4 box lasagna noodles, broken into small pieces

When we really want to please our MetroFreshuals, we'll put Beef Lasagna Soup on the menu. If they happen to visit the website, or read the daily email, they'll literally come from all over Metro Atlanta for a bowl or a quart. My friend John once came in to get a quart to go to share with his partner, Thomas. In theory, this was a sweet, nice idea. In practice, it didn't work because John had eaten the whole quart before Thomas walked through the door!

I always tell people, "It tastes surprisingly like lasagna!" And it's a soup! It's actually MUCH easier to make than lasagna, and just as delicious.

DIRECTIONS

1. Heat olive oil on the bottom of a 10 quart stock pot.

2. Add ground beef and brown. Cook down until some of the grease from the beef has evaporated. Pour beef into a colander to drain grease and put back into pan.

3. Add onion, carrots, celery, and garlic and sauté over medium heat until onions are translucent.

4. Add red wine and Italian seasoning. Add tomatoes and vegetable stock and bring to a boil. Turn to medium low heat and continue to cook for about 30 minutes.

5. Increase heat and bring back to a boil and lasagna noodles and cook until tender.

6. Turn off heat and add cheese. Stir soup with a wooden spoon until cheese has melted. It will be nice and gooey – perfect for serving immediately.

7. Serve in soup bowl with garlic bread and maybe a Caesar salad. And then wait for your guests to ooh and ah!

Serves 10-12
Yield – about 5 quarts

INGREDIENTS

1 cup diced red onion

2 cups diced celery

2 cups diced carrots

2 cups sliced fresh okra

¼ cup olive oil

4-5 cloves minced fresh garlic

1 red pepper diced

1 TBS ground cumin

3 TBS Cajun seasoning

1 Tsp cayenne pepper (more or less depending on your taste)

1 1lb can diced tomatoes (this in not in a traditional gumbo. I know this, but I like a little tomato in my gumbo!)

4 quarts vegetable stock

6 links sliced smoked beef sausage (or pork andouille sausage)

1lb. peeled and deveined shrimp, rinsed with water and tails removed

½ cup chopped Italian parsley

The great thing about Cajun or Creole cuisine is the blend of flavors. Wikipedia tells me West African, French, German, Choctaw Indian, and Spanish culinary traditions are literally stewed into this rich one pot meal. Gumbos are as different as the kitchens from which they come. Mine uses only okra for thickening, so it's not as traditional as ones made with a roux or filé powder. Traditionally, gumbo is served over rice. I like it that way, but in today's carb-conscious world you'll be fine without it.

DIRECTIONS

1. Heat oil in bottom of 10 quart stock pot.

2. Toss in onions, carrots, and celery and sauté for about 3 minutes.

3. Add okra and continue to sauté, stirring occasionally until okra begins to get sticky.

4. Add dried spices and mix in thoroughly. Sautee for another 2-3 minutes.

5. Add vegetable stock and tomatoes and bring to a boil. Immediately turn down to a slow simmer and cook for about an hour until carrots are tender.

6. Add shrimp, sausage, and parsley. If desired, serve over basmati rice.

SERVINGS

Serves 10-12
Yield – about 5 quarts

INGREDIENTS

1 large diced red onion

2 cups diced carrots

2 cups diced celery

¼ cup olive oil

2 28oz. cans
diced tomatoes

¼ cup of southwest
seasoning (Emeril has a
good one) OR you can use
chili powder

8 diced chicken thighs
or meat from 1 cooked
whole chicken

4 quarts chicken stock

1 12oz. bag tortilla
chips, crushed

2 cups shredded cheddar
jack cheese

1 bunch chopped cilantro
(if desired)

1 ripe but firm avocado

This is a deliciously cheesy, rich Mexican chicken soup. It's super easy and is a favorite with the MetroFresh crowd. Ok, so maybe it's not the *healthiest* thing we serve, but splurging once in a while makes life grand!

DIRECTIONS

1. Heat oil in the bottom of a 10 quart stock pot.

2. Sauté onions, carrots, and celery for 3-4 minutes until onions are tender.

3. Add southwest seasoning and continue to sauté for another two minutes.

4. Add tomatoes and chicken stock and bring to a boil. Immediately turn down to a slow simmer.

5. Add chicken and cook for about an hour.

6. Add crushed tortillas and cook for another 15 minutes or so. Stir occasionally so they don't stick to the bottom of the pot.

7. Stir in cheese and cilantro. Serve when cheese has melted. Top with sliced avocado and cilantro.

Sara Hanna Photography

Salads

Vegan and Vegetarian
Salads with Protein

SERVINGS

Yield – 1 Quart

INGREDIENTS

1 large shallot

4 cups fresh basil

½ cup Dijon mustard

¼ cup fresh lemon juice

¼ cup white
balsamic vinegar

3 cups blended oil (EVOO/
canola blend – you may
use canola, but don't
use all EVOO)

Kosher salt and
pepper to taste

So, this is MetroFresh's "secret" weapon. It's the only dressing we use for our green salads — and no one ever asks for ranch! We've been asked more times than I can count for the recipe. I'm not going to lie to you, it's not a cheapo dressing. But if you happen to have a big basil plant on your patio, or if you go to a farmer's market and can get LOTS of basil for not too much dough, then you'll be ahead of the game. Those little tiny packs with three leaves of basil for $1.99 you buy at the grocery store are worthless in this recipe.

You'll also need a food processor to really make this good.

DIRECTIONS

1. Fill food processor with fresh basil and chop with shallot until basil is fully pulverized.

2. Add in Dijon mustard, lemon juice and balsamic.

3. With food processor on, drizzle in oil and blend until emulsified (Adding too much oil will cause the dressing to separate over a few hours. It's not the end of the world if you do, but it'll take a little shaking before using).

4. Salt and pepper to taste.

5. Basil vinaigrette may be made ahead of time and kept refrigerated for up to 1 week. The dressing will turn a little darker over the week, but not to worry, it's still good – just a little oxidation of the basil.

FIVE HERB FIELD GREENS WITH BASIL VINAIGRETTE

SERVINGS

INGREDIENTS

2 bags triple washed field greens

2 TBS cup chopped chives

1 bunch chopped Italian parsley leaves

About ¼ cup chopped basil

2 TBS chopped dill

2 TBS chopped mint

(note – the herbs are more or less depending on your preference.)

1 cup dried cranberries or 1 cup fresh blueberries (or both)

½ cup toasted chopped pecans

1 pint sliced raw mushrooms (optional)

This salad is a little more work, but worth the effort. Its flavor is astounding and just sort of tastes like summer. It's the perfect salad to make when you have your own herb garden and are looking for something to do with all those fresh herbs.

DIRECTIONS

1. Toss all ingredients in a large salad bowl. Serve dressing on the side.

SLICED GRANNY SMITH APPLES, BLEU CHEESE AND SWEET/SPICY TOASTED WALNUTS

INGREDIENTS

1-2 packages of triple washed greens or 3-4 heads artisan greens of different color, washed and spun dried

1 large sliced Granny Smith apple

½ cup crumbled bleu cheese

1 cup walnuts

2 TBS extra virgin olive oil

1 TBS Jamaican jerk seasoning

2 TBS light brown sugar

Kosher salt to taste

DIRECTIONS

1. Prepare walnuts ahead of time. Preheat oven to 350. Toss walnuts in a bowl with brown sugar, Jamaican jerk seasoning, olive oil, and a little kosher salt. Coat nuts evenly. Spread on a cookie sheet and place in oven for about 10 minutes. Allow to cool.

2. Place lettuce in a bowl (or arrange on individual plates). Arrange sliced apple around in a pinwheel pattern on top of greens. Sprinkle crumbled bleu cheese and walnuts on top. Serve with basil vinaigrette dressing.

FIELD GREEN SALAD WITH METROFRESH BASIL VINAIGRETTE

SERVINGS

Serves 6-8

INGREDIENTS

Simple berries, mango and goat cheese

1-2 packages of triple washed greens or 3-4 heads artisan greens of different color, washed and spun dried

1 cup fresh sliced strawberries

½ pint fresh blackberries

½ pint fresh raspberries

1 diced mango

½ cup crumbled goat cheese (or feta)

This is our go to daily salad. We use curly artisan greens that have great depth of color and lots of natural "green" flavor. The secret is in the basil vinaigrette, which is so flavorful you don't even have to add anything to the greens, but for a pretty starter salad on a plate, or for a big bowl salad for a party, here are some suggestions.

DIRECTIONS

1. Place greens in a large salad bowl and arrange fruit on the top of the greens.

2. Crumble goat cheese on top.

3. Toss with a small amount of your basil vinaigrette. Do not over dress.

INGREDIENTS

1 bag baby arugula

¾ cup trimmed
oyster mushrooms

¾ cup trimmed
shitake mushrooms

extra virgin olive oil

2-3 fresh leeks, sliced
and washed

canola oil for leeks

shaved parmesan

Baby arugula, or "rocket" arugula, is in. The hipsters in New York City can't get enough of it. The delicate leaves have this incredible exotic, peppery taste without being bitter. This salad may be tossed, or composed on individual plates for a more formal dinner.

DIRECTIONS

1. For dressing – Use MetroFresh Basil Vinaigrette (See page 54) or just toss with a little lemon juice, a good olive oil, salt and pepper

2. Toss trimmed mushrooms in a few table spoons of olive oil and a little salt. Arrange on sheet tray and place in 350 oven for 5-7 minutes until just tender. Remove and chill.

3. Two ways to crisp leeks – one is messy but great, the other is easier but not quite as good. METHOD 1: Heat about 2 cups canola oil in 4 quart sauce pan (you want the pot to be large enough so that oil doesn't boil over (oil is hot enough when one leek slice bubbles when dropped in). Add leeks in small amounts to hot oil (caution – there is a high water content in leeks, so the hot oil will bubble rapidly and it's very dangerous! Wait for steam to die down before adding each load of leeks). You should be able to cook all leeks in one batch. Use slotted spoon to stir. When leeks are golden brown, remove from oil and onto paper towel to blot the oil. Sprinkle a small amount of Kosher salt over and set aside. METHOD 2: Toss leeks in a small amount of oil with some salt and cook on shallow pan in oven at 350 until brown. Much less messy, but not as exciting!

4. Toss arugula, leeks and mushrooms in large bowl. Drizzle on just enough dressing to coat arugula leaves – don't over dress. Top with shaved parmesan.

OR : Place a small mound of arugula on a salad plate and arrange mushrooms, leeks and parmesan on top. Drizzle with small amount of dressing.

OPTIONAL : Top with pomegranate seeds, dried cranberries, or sun dried tomatoes for a little color.

GINGER APPLE BEETS

SERVINGS

Serves 6

INGREDIENTS

6 large gold, red, or
candy-striped beets,
peeled and diced into 1
inch cubes

2 diced Granny
Smith apples

1 bunch chopped cilantro
(or mint if you don't
like cilantro)

1 bunch chopped
green onion

3 TBS fresh ginger

¼ cup orange juice

2 TBS seedy Dijon mustard

2 TBS maple syrup

1 cup blended olive/
canola oil

I always thought if I ever became famous for being a chef, it would be because of my MetroFresh Basil Vinaigrette or Ginger Apple Beets. First of all, you can't really go wrong with fresh beets as far as I'm concerned. Over the years, I've noticed the "I hate beets" crowd has dwindled to a few after they try any beet salad at MetroFresh. Most people who don't like beets have only ever had canned, processed beets on a salad bar at Applebee's. I learned to eat fresh beets as a child from my Grampe's garden in Rochester. I've always loved them. I'm pretty sure that if you serve this salad at a party, your guests are going to go wild!

DIRECTIONS

1. Preheat oven to 350 degrees. Toss beets in a small amount of blended oil and a little kosher salt. Place on a cookie sheet and bake in the oven for 15-20 minutes. I like my beets a little al dente, but cook longer if you like them a little softer. Remove from the oven and allow them to cool thoroughly.

2. Place beets and diced apples in a salad bowl with chopped cilantro and green onion.

3. For the dressing – pulverize ginger in food processor. Add mustard and continue to blend. Drizzle in maple syrup, orange juice and oil until dressing has emulsified.

4. Toss dressing on beets and apples and serve immediately. This salad can be fully prepared ahead of time and allowed to sit until ready to serve. It's even great the next day.

5. Note – Red beets are fine to use, but because they "bleed" the apples will turn a lovely pinkish purple. It's all good, but if you want a clean look, use golden or candy striped beets.

TEX MEX CHOP CHOP WITH AVOCADO LIME SOUR CREAM DRESSING

SERVINGS

Serves 8-10

INGREDIENTS

3 heads chopped romaine

1 bunch chopped cilantro

1 diced hothouse cucumber

1 cup matchstick or shredded carrots

1 10oz can rinsed black beans

1 pint halved grape tomatoes

1 cup raw corn cut from the cob

1 bunch chopped green onion

1 diced mango

6 eggs

2 ripe but firm avocadoes

1 cup shredded cheddar/jack or sharp cheddar cheese

¼ cup olive oil

For the Dressing –

2 TBS diced red onion

2 cloves of garlic

½ cup sour cream

1 ripe avocado

2 TBS cilantro

2 TBS fresh lime juice

2 TBS rice wine vinegar

½ cup blended oil

1 tsp Sriracha (optional)

I believe in this salad. Along with our Thai Chop Chop, it's one of my favorites. You can add sliced chicken breast to the salad and you'll have a whole meal.

DIRECTIONS

1. Start by scrambling eggs. Heat a medium sized non-stick skillet on high heat with about 2 TBS Olive Oil until oil is just smoking. Pour half the scrambled egg mixture onto the bottom of the pan. Sprinkle with a little salt and pepper. It should bubble up and start cooking right away if skillet is hot enough. Cook until edges are brown and "omelet" can be flipped without breaking. Turn eggs just once and cook for another minute or so. Slide onto a cookie sheet and reheat the pan with the remaining oil. Repeat the previous step with the second batch. Remove from heat and put both omelets in the refrigerator to cool.

2. Meanwhile, toss all other salad ingredients in a large salad bowl. When omelets have cooled, cut into 1 inch squares and add to the salad. Toss thoroughly.

FOR THE DRESSING:

1. Place onion, garlic and cilantro in food processor or blender and pulverize. Add, avocado, sour cream and blend. Add lime juice, vinegar and Sriracha (if desired) then slowly add oil to emulsify.

2. Before serving, add diced avocado to the salad and toss with dressing.

OPTIONAL: Add sliced grilled chicken, Andouille sausage, or pulled pork. You might also like a little crunchiness, so add some crushed tortilla chips.

Sara Hanna Photography

SERVINGS

Serves 6-8

INGREDIENTS

4 bunches of kale, washed

3-4 red pears

1 cup golden raisins

1 cup halved walnuts

½ cup while
balsamic vinegar

½ cup honey or
maple syrup

½ cup blended olive/
canola oil

Kosher or sea salt to taste

*Optional Ingredients:
apples, pears, seasonal
berries, mango, nuts,
orange segments

Kale, it turns out, is a "super food." It's packed with essential natural vitamins and minerals. Marinated for a few hours before serving in white balsamic dressing and a little blended olive/canola oil with a touch of honey, the kale "tenderizes" without losing its beneficial qualities. We make it many different ways, so I encourage you to experiment, but more often than not we'll add a couple different fresh seasonal fruits and some kind of nut.

DIRECTIONS

1. Rinse and dry kale. Remove center ribs and discard. Chop leaves into fine pieces and place into a large bowl. Use sharp knife and be careful not to mash the greens.

2. Drizzle honey or maple syrup over the kale and add vinegar, oil and a little salt. Massage kale with your hands to mix the liquid ingredients.

3. Add fruit and nuts – toss lightly.

4. For the best tasting salad, cover and place in refrigerator for 30-60 minutes. Toss once again and serve. The longer you let the greens sit, the tenderer they will be. The salad loses some of its shape, but what it loses in prettiness, it gains in flavor.

VEGGIE "TRAIL MIX"

SERVINGS

Serves 6-8

INGREDIENTS

1 bunch broccoli finely chopped, stems removed

1 head cauliflower finely chopped

4-5 diced carrots and lightly chopped in the food processor

1 cup dried cranberries

For the dressing –

½ cup seedy Dijon mustard

½ cup honey

½ cup fresh orange Juice

1 cup olive oil/canola oil blend

Kosher Salt to taste

Many items on the MetroFresh menu make frequent appearances because our regular customers love them so much. Veggie "Trail Mix" is one of these items. It's a salad that just simply tastes like "health." There's not much mystery here; it's pretty straightforward. It's just crunchy goodness. I created this salad many years ago when we first opened, and I called it Trail Mix because it reminded me of my Aunt Ginny's bag of trail mix she'd take on hikes. So there you go...

DIRECTIONS

1. Finely chop cauliflower and broccoli with sharp knife. Chop carrots lightly in food processor. Toss in a bowl with cranberries and dressing. Serve immediately or refrigerate. Will keep well for up to two days.

OPTIONS: Add walnuts, pecans, toasted pumpkin seeds, bleu cheese crumbles.

PEACH CAPRESE SALAD

SERVINGS

Serves 6-8

INGREDIENTS

6-8 fresh peaches (make sure they are nice and ripe, but not mushy), diced into 1 inch cubes

2lbs. fresh mozzarella

1 cup grape or cherry tomatoes cut in half

1 diced hothouse cucumber

¼ cup basil chiffonade (basil ribbons)

2 TBS white balsamic vinegar

½ cup extra virgin olive oil

Kosher salt and cracked pepper to taste

Ok, so in my mind there is nothing better than a fresh, local peach. Of course, living in Atlanta means a famous Georgia peach. But growing up in the farm country of Western New York, we had pretty darn good peaches too. This is such a great use of fresh peaches and is a twist on a traditional caprese.

DIRECTIONS

1. Wash and, if desired, peel the peaches. I don't peel them because I like the skin, but if you decide to be like me and use the skin, make sure you wash them well.

2. In a large shallow bowl, put down a layer of sliced peaches.

3. Top the peaches with a layer of cubed fresh mozzarella, cucumber, and tomato and then sprinkle with a basil, salt and pepper. Repeat layers.

4. Drizzle white balsamic over the salad and then olive oil. Let sit for up to an hour, toss and serve.

MEDITERRANEAN STRAWBERRY AND CUCUMBER SALAD WITH MINT AND FETA

SERVINGS

Serves about 6

INGREDIENTS

2 pints
strawberries – rinsed
clean and sliced

2 hothouse cucumbers.
These do not have to be
peeled or seeded and give
a nice deep green contrast
to the berries. Cut into half
inch cubes.

½ - 1 cup of good feta
diced into ¼ in squares

4-5 sprigs of
mint, chopped

2 TBS white
balsamic vinegar

¼ cup extra virgin olive oil

Kosher salt and
pepper to taste

The sweetness of fresh strawberries, the coolness of hothouse cucumbers, the brightness of fresh mint, and savory feta combine for a delicious summer salad that's great on a picnic or a back yard BBQ.

DIRECTIONS

1. Use a shallow medium size bowl for this salad. Put a layer of sliced berries on the bottom of the bowl.

2. Next put about half as many cucumbers, a fourth of the feta, and a sprinkle of mint, salt and pepper. Repeat each layer until all the berries, cucumber, mint and feta are finished. Make sure the top layer has lots of contrasting colors for presentation.

3. Drizzle white balsamic and EVO over the top of the salad covering as much as possible. Don't worry about tossing the salad. The "dressing" will mix on its own with the first spoonful. Serve immediately and enjoy.

ALTERNATIVES: Use basil instead of mint. Use fresh mozzarella instead of feta. Add chopped green onions.

SERVINGS

Serves 4

INGREDIENTS

3 heads Belgian endive sliced lengthwise

1 roasted beet (golden or candy striped is best as they don't "bleed") cut into small pieces

1 tsp chopped fresh tarragon

2 TBS chopped Italian parsley

Salt and pepper to taste

For the Dressing –

½ cup dried cherries

½ cup white balsamic vinegar

1 TBS Dijon mustard

1 cup canola/ olive oil blend

In the fall of 2014, I put together a great dinner at the restaurant with my friend Victoria Price, daughter of famed actor Vincent. The idea was to create a menu inspired by the Vincent Price Signature Wine Collection and his landmark 1965 cookbook A TREASURY OF GREAT RECIPES. The cookbook was a collection of recipes from famous restaurants of the day from all over the world. So in full disclosure, this recipe was inspired by a similar dish from Antoine's in New Orleans,

DIRECTIONS

1. Put cherries in a small sauce pan and cover with white balsamic. Cook over medium heat for about 20 minutes or until cherries are very tender. Cool in refrigerator.

2. Put cherry and vinegar in the food processor and blend until cherries a pulverized. Add Dijon mustard. Arrange salad on individual plates and drizzle with dressing (the salad can also be tossed and served family style).

SERVINGS

Serves 6

INGREDIENTS

1 large butternut squash peeled and diced into 1 inch cubes

2 bunches chopped broccolini (or broccoli crowns if broccolini is too bitter for you)

1 head shredded Napa cabbage

½ cup chopped fresh basil

½ cup dried cranberries

1 lemon

½ cup maple syrup or honey

½ cup extra virgin olive oil

Kosher salt and cracked pepper to taste

This is a perfect fall/winter salad. Like most of our salads at MetroFresh, we make ingredient decisions based as much on color as we do on taste. It's really what gives us these unique combinations and draws our diners in. Your eyes will taste this salad with the bright yellow/orange butternut squash combined with the deep green of the broccolini and the ruby red of the cranberries before you even put it in your mouth. Serve this with a grilled pork chop or baked chicken and you'll have a delicious and comforting winter meal.

DIRECTIONS

1. Preheat oven to 350.

2. Toss cubed butternut squash in a little oil and kosher salt. Bake on cookie sheet for about 15 minutes until squash is just cooked through. Do not overcook the squash as the salad will become mushy.

3. Toss chopped broccolini in a little olive oil and bake at 350 for about 7 minutes on a cookie sheet.

4. Cool squash and broccolini in the refrigerator.

5. Toss squash, broccolini, cabbage, cranberries, and basil in a bowl. Squeeze the juice from one lemon over salad.

6. Toss with maple syrup and olive oil. Salt and pepper to taste. Serve immediately, or return to refrigerator for up to a day.

RED QUINOA SALAD WITH FRESH RAW CORN, GRAPE TOMATOES, AVOCADO — LIME CILANTRO DRESSING

SERVINGS

Serves 6

INGREDIENTS

1 cup red (or white) quinoa rinsed several times under cold water

About 2 cups grape or cherry tomatoes halved or quartered

1 cup raw corn cut from the husk (about 3 ears)

2 ripe but firm avocadoes – diced into ½ in squares

1 hot house cucumber diced in ½ inch squares

1 bunch green onion (optional) or ½ cup finely diced red onion

FOR DRESSING

1 bunch fresh cilantro

¼ cup lime juice (orange juice or lemon juice can be used also)

¾ cup Blended Oil (or canola oil)

2 TBS honey

salt and pepper to taste

I created this recipe for a cooking class a few years ago. Quinoa is a super food. It's an ancient grain from the Andes Mountains in South America and is known for its high protein content. The red variety is just a little crunchier and nuttier than its whiter cousin. Make sure the quinoa is cooked through but not too moist when you're making the salad.

FOR THE SALAD

1. Put rinsed quinoa in medium sauce pan and add water. For 1 cup of quinoa, use 2 cups of salted water. Bring water to a boil, cover and reduce heat to a low simmer. The grain will absorb water and be ready in about 10-15 minutes. Fluff with a fork and pour into a shallow bowl. Cool through in the refrigerator. Dressing and quinoa can be done a day in advance and kept chilled.

2. In medium bowl add tomatoes, corn, onion (if desired), and avocado to the chilled quinoa. Toss lightly with dressing and salt and pepper to taste. Serve immediately. If you are taking salad on a picnic either leave out avocado and add just before serving.

FOR THE DRESSING

1. Chop cilantro in food processor and add lime juice.

2. Add a squeeze or two of honey and then drizzle in oil until emulsified.

3. Add a little salt. Set aside.

OPTIONS: Add diced mango, peaches, nectarines, and/or black beans.

CLEMENTINE ORANGE AND ASPARAGUS SALAD WITH SHAVED FENNEL AND BASIL

SERVINGS

Serves 6

INGREDIENTS

2 bunches fresh asparagus – for thin asparagus, pealing is not necessary. For thick asparagus, I like to peal the bottom of the stalk. Cut into ¼ - ½ inch pieces.

4-5 sectioned clementine oranges. You can also use navel, blood orange, or tangerines, as long as there are no seeds

1 large shaved fennel bulb (reserve fronds for later)

¼ cup chopped fresh basil

¼ cup real maple syrup

½ cup EVOO

Juice from 1 lemon

salt and pepper to taste

In the MetroFresh kitchen, the trick is to combine basically the same list of ingredients in different ways to come up with different tastes. Between the three of us on the creative team, it's almost a competition. I love asparagus salads. If I had more financial sense than artistic sense, this salad would never make it on the MetroFresh menu. But I don't. I just love to create what I want when I want it. I think this one is a winner.

DIRECTIONS

1. To blanch asparagus – bring medium pot of very salty water to a boil. Add chopped asparagus and cook about 2 minutes – you want asparagus to be al dente. Toss in ice bath and chill thoroughly.

2. To roast asparagus – Toss in EVOO and a little kosher salt – enough to cover. Put in single layer on cookie sheet. Cook in pre-heated 350 degree oven for about 5 minutes. Do not overcook. Chill in refrigerator.

3. Cut off fennel fronds and put aside. Halve bulb and with sharp knife (or mandolin, if you have one) shave fennel into very thin shards.

4. Toss asparagus, oranges, fennel, and basil in medium bowl.

5. Add lemon juice, maple syrup, and EVOO and toss until mixed.

6. Salt and pepper to taste.

7. Chop a small amount of fennel fronds and sprinkle on top of salad before serving. For a little extra zip, add a touch of lemon zest.

OPTIONS: Try roasted, fresh haricot vert, roasted Brussels sprouts, fresh English peas

SERVINGS

Serves about 6

FOR THE CHIPS

12 white corn tortillas cut into six pieces

olive oil spray

Kosher salt

FOR THE GUACAMOLE

2 ripe mangoes

½ cup finely diced red onion

1 minced garlic clove (optional)

2-3 jalapeno peppers, finely diced

¼ cup chopped cilantro

2 ripe but not soft avocadoes

2 TBS olive oil

juice from 2 limes

salt and pepper to taste

On catering gigs, I often fall back on this amazing guacamole. I also make it all the time at the lake after a long day on the boat when our campers are hungry. It doesn't last long.

Mostly I use blue corn tortillas, but if you want to be super healthy and make your own chips, I've included them in the recipe.

DIRECTIONS

1. Stack tortillas and cut into six pieces. Place on baking sheet in single layer and spay both sides with olive oil. Lightly salt and bake in pre-heated 350 degree oven until crispy, about 12-15 minutes

2. Peel and dice mango into ¼ inch cubes. Add onion, garlic if desired, and jalapeno. Toss with cilantro, lime juice and olive oil.

3. Add diced avocado and lightly toss with mango salsa. Salt and pepper to taste. Serve immediately with chips. This makes a great topping for grilled salmon, peppery steak, or pork chops.

HELPFUL HINT: Cut the avocado in half and remove the seed. With a butter knife (or "spreader") make a cross-hatch in the flesh of the avocado and simply scoop right into the bowl.

INGREDIENTS

2 lbs. cooked farro

1 diced hot house cucumber

1 cup diced carrots

1 cup chopped celery

1 cup chopped raw broccoli

½ cup chopped walnuts

½ cup golden raisins

½ cup dried cranberries

¼ cup chopped fresh mint

¼ cup chopped basil

¼ cup chopped fresh Italian parsley

½ cup chopped green onions (optional)

salt and pepper to taste

FOR THE DRESSING

½ cup seedy Dijon mustard

½ cup ruby red grapefruit juice (fresh is best if you don't mind spending the money)

2 TBS maple syrup

1 cup blended olive/canola oil (Don't use 100% EVOO in this dressing)

Farro is one of my favorite grains. It was originally cultivated in Italy in the dark ages and is a staple of Italian cooking. I sometimes describe it as whole wheat barley because in the cooking process, it puffs up like barley. This salad takes advantage of the natural crunchiness and nuttiness of farro, using fresh raw vegetables and colorful fruit to make a gorgeous salad. I also use lots of fresh herbs so it's almost like a tabbouleh. Take this to your next summer cookout instead of pasta and you'll be the talk of the pool deck.

DIRECTIONS

1. Cook farro according to directions. I cook it like pasta. If you have a rolling boil when you put the farro in, it should take about 10 minutes. Don't overcook. Rinse farro in a colander thoroughly to cool it down. Or drain water and place cooked farro in the refrigerator to cool.

2. Combine all ingredients in a large salad bowl and toss with dressing. It's ready to serve immediately, or you can put it back in the fridge and serve later. I sometimes take this to our lake house and it lasts all weekend!

SERVINGS

Serves 6

INGREDIENTS

6 large vine ripe tomatoes

1 finely chopped
jalapeno pepper

¼ cup finely
diced red onion

2 TBS fresh lime juice

1 TBS extra virgin olive oil

2 TBS chopped cilantro

Kosher salt to taste

We use Pico De Gallo (or salsa, as some would call it) to top just about anything at MetroFresh. It's great on our Smoked Gouda Grits and Eggs (page 19), Sarah's Breakfast Special (page 10) or to top grilled fish. Make it ahead of time and store it in the fridge for up to three days — after that it'll breakdown and not be great.

DIRECTIONS

1. Wash and dry the tomatoes. You're going to make what the French call a concasse in which you only use the outside meat and skin of the tomato. The easiest way to do this is by quartering the tomato and taking you knife and scraping out the inside flesh and seeds, leaving only the outside skin. You can discard the tomato meat, or save it and make tomato jam (see recipe page 17).

2. Dice the remaining skin into ¼ inch pieces. Toss in bowl with jalapeno, red onion, and cilantro. Pour in lime juice and drizzle a little EVO over the bowl. Toss with a little kosher salt to taste. Serve immediately or put in sealed container and store for up to three days.

FRESH PEACH CURRY "WALDORF" CHICKEN SALAD WITH GOLDEN RAISINS, WALNUTS AND MAPLE DIJON DRESSING

INGREDIENTS

4 boneless/skinless chicken breasts

4 – 5 fresh peaches, washed and diced

1 cup diced celery

½ cup golden raisins

½ cup roughly chopped walnuts

½ cup chopped Italian or curly parsley

¼ cup chopped fresh mint

Salt and pepper to taste

FOR THE DRESSING

½ cup seedy Dijon mustard

¼ cup maple syrup

½ cup fresh grapefruit juice

2 TBS toasted curry powder

1 cup blended oil

Again with the peaches! I'm a little like my mother in this way. When something is in season, it should be used…daily! I love curry chicken salad, but I realize it's not for everyone. If you have a finicky eater in your bunch, make this salad the same way and simply omit the curry powder. Also, just FYI, this is great with Granny Smith apples as well.

DIRECTIONS

1. To make this dressing properly, you're going to need to toast the curry just a bit. Don't panic. It's easy. Simply put curry powder on the bottom of a very small skillet and heat over medium high flame until it begins to smoke just a bit. Set aside.

2. Use a food processor to make the dressing. Add curry powder to mustard and with blender on, drizzle in grapefruit juice, maple syrup and finally, your blended oil. Set aside.

3. Place chicken breasts on baking sheet and lightly coat with olive oil and salt. Bake in 350 oven for about 35 minutes, to an internal temp of 165. Chill thoroughly. Dice into 1in. cubes.

4. Toss chicken in bowl with the diced peaches (skin on is fine, but you can peel if desired), celery, raisins, walnuts, and herbs and toss thoroughly. Add dressing and toss once again to coat. Salt and pepper to taste. Serve immediately or refrigerate. Depending on ripeness of peaches, the salad with last a day or two.

5. This salad works perfectly without chicken if you are vegetarian. You might also try it with farro, quinoa, wheat berries or any other hardy grain.

THAI PEANUT CHICKEN AND CABBAGE SALAD

INGREDIENTS

4 cooked and diced boneless/skinless chicken breast

2 cups shredded Napa cabbage

1 cup shredded purple cabbage

½ cup matchstick carrots

½ cup chopped cilantro

½ cup chopped mint

¼ cup chopped Thai basil (use regular basil if Thai basil is too hard to find)

½ cup dry roasted peanuts (or if you live near a Trader Joes, use their chili/lime cashews)

½ cup tiny diced red pepper for topping

Kosher salt or soy sauce to taste (soy sauce will make this recipe not gluten free)

FOR THE DRESSING

2 TBS fresh ginger

1 cup sweet chili sauce

½ cup peanut butter

¼ cup rice wine vinegar

¾ cup blended olive/canola oil

One of the best things about Thai food is being able to taste each individual flavor. This salad has so many great tastes that it'll explode in your mouth! This particular chicken salad is best to make and serve immediately to preserve the integrity of each individual flavor. But don't throw out leftovers. It will be good the next day — just not as distinct.

FOR THE DRESSING

1. Pulverize ginger in food processor.

2. Add peanut butter and sweet chili sauce and blend.

3. Add rice wine vinegar and continue to blend.

4. Add blended oil until dressing is smooth.

FOR THE SALAD

1. Toss all salad ingredients into a bowl and mix thoroughly. Add dressing and coat completely. Serve immediately or refrigerate for up to three hours. Salad is good for the next day, but the cabbage will begin to breakdown.

FIESTA CHICKEN SALAD

SERVINGS

Serves 8-10

I love this particular chicken salad because it's so colorful. Like everything we make at MetroFresh, color is so important. It has a particularly Mexican flare and can be perfect for a summer picnic or pool party.

INGREDIENTS

2lbs. diced boneless/ skinless chicken breast

4 ears of fresh corn, with kernels sliced from the cob

1 10oz. can black beans, rinsed under cold water and drained

2 diced mangos

1 cup diced celery

½ cup finely diced red onion

½ cup matchstick carrots

1 pint cherry or grape tomatoes cut in half

1 bunch chopped cilantro

2-3 TBS olive oil

Salt and pepper to taste

For the Dressing –

1 cup sour cream

½ cup lo-fat olive oil mayonnaise

1 ripe avocado

½ cup fresh lime juice

½ cup blended olive/ canola oil

1 TBS Siracha or hot sauce (more or less to taste)

DIRECTIONS

1. To cook chicken, preheat oven to 350. Place chicken breast on sheet pan and cook for about 35 minutes or until internal temperature reaches 165 – do not overcook. Chill before dicing.

2. Toss corn with a little olive oil, salt and pepper and place on baking sheet. Cook in 350 oven for about 15 minutes until it just begins to brown. Chill.

3. Mix all ingredients for salad in large mixing bowl.

4. Make dressing in food processor. First put the meat of the avocado and blend. Add lime juice and continue blending. Add sour cream, mayo, oil, and hot sauce. Salt and pepper to taste.

5. Toss dressing on salad and serve immediately. This salad can be made ahead of time, but the avocado will turn slightly brown, so don't wait too long to enjoy.

OPTION: Add crispy corn tortilla chips and shredded cheddar/jack cheese!

SERVINGS

Serves 6-8 as a main course

INGREDIENTS

2 lbs. London broil steak –
marinated for 4-8 hours,
grilled and thinly sliced

2 heads chopped romaine

1 pint grape tomatoes

1 diced mango

1 cup shredded carrots

1 bag baby arugula

1 cup bean sprouts (optional)

½ cup chopped cilantro

¼ cup chopped mint

¼ cup chopped Thai basil

¼ cup chopped green onions

For the dressing and
marinade for the beef

3 TBS minced fresh ginger

1 clove garlic

1 bunch cilantro

¼ cup lime juice

½ cup sweet chili sauce

1 cup blended olive/
canola oil

¼ cup low sodium soy sauce

2 TBS honey (or refined
white sugar)

Yes, we're back to Thailand! Sorry, I can't help myself. These are distinct flavors that transport you to the wilds of Southeast Asia without having to leave the comfort of your own kitchen. I hope you enjoy it as much as I do!

DIRECTIONS

1. Make the dressing first. Peel ginger and garlic. Pulverize in food processor. Add cilantro and continue to blend. Add in lime juice, soy sauce, chili sauce, honey and blend. Drizzle in oil until mixture is emulsified.

2. Place meat in a Ziploc bag with about ½ cup of the dressing and return to the refrigerator for at least 4 hours.

3. Grill steak to desired temperature and chill thoroughly. When chilled, you can slice the steak in thin 2 inch strips or 1 inch cubes.

4. Prepare the rest of the salad ahead of time, or when you're about to serve. As long as the meat is fully chilled, you can put it all together and toss with dressing just before serving.

LOBSTERCADOES (OR CRABACADOS)

SERVINGS

Serves 4-6

INGREDIENTS

1 lbs. lobster or crab meat

½ cup diced celery

¼ cup diced green onion or 1 TBS finely diced shallot

2 TBS chopped fresh dill

½ cup lo-fat olive oil mayo

1 TBS smooth Dijon mustard

1 tsp Siracha (optional)

Salt and pepper to taste

Paprika for dusting

1 lime

¼ cup olive oil

2 – 3 avocadoes cut in half, seed removed.

Once in a while, when we're feeling generous and have the time, we make lobster or crab salad and serve it on top of a half avocado. It's a bit decadent, but for a nice summer lunch, it's the perfect "entrée." Serve it with a caprese salad on the side and you have a beautiful plate. Lobster meat is hard to come by and is a bit of a pain to "create" from whole lobsters, but it's worth it. If you don't want to go to all the trouble, substitute whole lump crab instead.

DIRECTIONS

1. Combine lobster or crab meat, celery, onion, and dill in a bowl. Toss "dry" ingredients with mayo, mustard and, if desired, Siracha. Salt and pepper to taste.

2. Choose a ripe but slightly firm avocado. Cut avocado in half and remove seed. Make a small slice on the rounded side of the avocado to give it stability on the plate.

3. Mix lime juice and olive oil in a small bowl and pour in a saucer. Dip open side of avocado in oil and then place a scoop of salad on top (This will prevent the avocado from oxidizing immediately, turning it an unpleasant brown color). Position on plate (use some spinach of greens as a base if desired). Sprinkle a little paprika on top. Serve immediately. Can be kept in the refrigerator for up to 3 hours before serving.

Sara Hanna Photography

RECIPES

Dinner Time

INGREDIENTS

1lb ground chuck

1lb sweet Italian sausage
(bulk or casings removed)

1 28oz can
chopped tomatoes

1 28oz can tomato sauce

1 6oz can tomato paste

½ cup yellow onion

½ cup diced yellow pepper

½ cup diced red pepper

4-5 chopped garlic cloves

2 tbs olive oil

2 tbs Italian seasoning

1 tsp fennel seeds

1 lb linguini

Salt and pepper to taste

My nana was a great cook. One of my favorites was a Bolognese that was rich and flavorful, but totally accessible. I looked forward to it every time we visited her house in Rochester, NY. She served it over linguini with some crusty garlic bread and a tossed salad and it was the kind of meal you dream about. I've put my own spin on it, and you should do yours, but here's the recipe I use which will serve about 10 people. When I make it at home, I serve some and freeze the rest in small plastic containers for easy dinners when I don't feel like cooking.

DIRECTIONS

1. Heat a small amount of olive oil on medium high heat in a large saucepan.

2. Add diced onions, peppers and garlic and sauté until onions are translucent and peppers are very tender.

3. Add ground meat and sausage and brown through.

4. Add Italian seasoning and fennel seeds. Simmer for a few minutes on medium heat.

5. Stir in tomato paste and the equivalent amount of water. Add tomato sauce and chopped tomatoes. Simmer sauce covered for at least 1 hour, stirring occasionally.

6. Serve over linguini with shaved parmesan and a dollop of ricotta cheese if desired.

LIGHT SUMMER PASTA WITH FRESH VEGETABLES AND SPICY ITALIAN TURKEY SAUSAGE

SERVINGS

Serves 8

INGREDIENTS

1 medium size
zucchini - diced

1 yellow squash - diced

½ bunch asparagus, cut
into 1 inch pieces

2-3 cloves garlic

½ yellow or white
onion (Vidalia onions
are the best in the
summer), julienned

1 cup cherry or grape
tomatoes cut in half

1 small package
baby arugula

1 cup white wine

1 cup chicken broth

1 cup pasta water

3-5 hot Italian turkey
sausage – casings removed

Fresh mozzarella

Shaved parmesan cheese

Kosher salt

¼ cup extra virgin olive oil

1 box fusilli pasta (Or
penne/rigatoni)

I love this dish. Pasta in the spring and summer can seem so heavy and filling, but this light "Primavera" is incredibly satisfying without filling you up. Serve it with a crusty baguette and it's a one dish meal - you don't even need a salad. And the best part? Leftovers are great cold!

DIRECTIONS

1. Boil heavily salted pasta water. Cook as directed.

2. While pasta is boiling – heat olive oil in large skillet over medium high heat.

3. Crumble in turkey sausage out of the casing and sauté until brown.

4. Add onions and garlic and sauté for 1 minute or so.

5. Add vegetables and continue to cook for another minute.

6. Deglaze pan with white wine.

7. Turn up heat to high. Bring to boil and add about a cup of chicken stock and about a cup of pasta water (you can use a ladle and take it from the pasta pot while pasta is cooking.) Cook until squash is just tender and then add tomatoes and arugula. Salt to taste (you shouldn't have to add too much). Remove from heat.

8. Drain pasta and toss with vegetable/sausage mixture in large bowl. Top with fresh mozzarella and shaved parmesan and serve in pasta bowls.

9. On a hot summer night, I like using previously cooked pasta and tossing it with warm vegetable/sausage mixture. It's a refreshing, but not hot, dish. Serve with crusty baguette.

SERVINGS

To serve 4 people you'll need:

FOR THE CHICKEN

8 chicken thighs or 4 chicken breasts

1 cup finely chopped pecans

½ cup panko or plain breadcrumbs

½ cup flour

(To make a gluten free version of this dish, don't worry about breadcrumbs or flour – it works well with just the pecans!)

½ cup finely chopped fresh parsley

Cayenne pepper (just a pinch or more for a little kick)

1 egg

1 cup milk

Canola oil spray

Honey

Salt and pepper

FOR THE PESTO

1 bag (about 12 ounces) baby arugula

2 cloves garlic

Juice from 1 lemon

½ cup extra virgin olive oil

¼ cup honey

FOR THE ASPARAGUS

1 bunch asparagus (5 or 6 spears/person), trimmed and peeled

extra virgin olive oil

Kosher salt

A squeeze of lemon

Every MetroFresh recipe comes with the following caveat — WE DON'T REALLY USE RECIPES! I know, this doesn't help you, but amongst our creative team in the kitchen, we encourage an improv style of cooking. As Creator and Head Chef, I'll suggest something to my Executive Chef or our Assistant Chef, and they'll come up with their own version. My Pecan Chicken will be different from theirs and that's the idea. This dish appeared on our dinner menu one night, and the next day, there was a request in my inbox for the recipe! Hopefully you'll experiment and use this version as a jumping off point for your own creation. We served this dish hot, of course, but it would make a great chilled dinner for a summer picnic or outdoor concert!

DIRECTIONS FOR THE CHICKEN

1. Preheat Oven to 350. In a medium size bowl pour and mix all dry ingredients – pecans, flour, panko, cayenne pepper, and parsley. In another medium bowl, scramble 1 egg and mix in 1 cup of milk. Soak chicken in egg/milk mixture for five minutes (this can be done ahead of time and put in fridge for up to two hours). Dredge coated chicken through the well-mixed dry ingredients and place each piece of chicken on flat cooking sheet. Drizzle small amount of honey over each piece of chicken. Spray canola oil just to cover (don't need too much) and place in preheated oven. (Discard unused dry ingredients even though it's tempting to save them – you don't want raw chicken and egg hanging around to make you sick!)

2. All chicken is different, but thighs should take about 45 minutes to an hour to cook. You've got a little more room for error with thighs since they have a little more fat content and won't dry out too easily. Chicken breasts take a little less time but because they're leaner, it's easy to overcook them. The pecan crust should be lightly browned and internal temperature at the thickest part of the meat should be 165 degrees.

3. While the chicken is in the oven you can trim and peel the asparagus. I usually skip the peeling part because I don't mind the spines, but if you're trying to impress your friends, if you lightly peel the stalks they'll be a little tenderer. Brush with extra virgin olive oil and cook on very hot grill, turning spears until they are cooked to a nice crisp al dente (btw, grill marks make the asparagus look awesome!). Grilling usually takes about 3 minutes depending on thickness of asparagus. If you don't have a grill, just put asparagus on a cookie sheet and cook in a 350 oven for 7-10 minutes, depending on thickness. Sprinkle with kosher salt and a squeeze of lemon. Cook asparagus just before serving, or grill earlier and chill. Cold asparagus is the bomb!

FOR THE ARUGULA PESTO

1. In a food processor, chop 2 cloves of garlic (or a couple more if you like a garlicky pesto). Add arugula. With motor running squeeze in juice from 1 whole lemon. Drizzle in ½ cup of honey and about ½ cup of EVOO and salt to taste. The pesto should be the consistency of a thick salad dressing.

2. When chicken is done, place two thighs or one breast on a plate. Spoon just a dab of pesto on top of the chicken. Place 4 or 5 spears of asparagus on plate and serve with a lemon wedge.

COMPOSED DINNER SALAD WITH GRILLED STEAK OR CHICKEN BREAST

SERVINGS

Here's the recipe and amounts I'd use for four plates

INGREDIENTS

3 bunches butter lettuce, washed and dried

3 hard-boiled eggs, shelled and sliced

4 medium sized steamed red beets, diced

1 bunch green onions

1 pint halved cherry tomatoes

1 peeled, seeded and sliced cucumber

½ cup crumbled gorgonzola cheese (or any kind of good crumbly bleu cheese)

4 filet mignons (Or if you don't want to spend the money, you can use any cut of steak you like. London broil works well if you have time to properly marinate it)

Or – 4 skinless/boneless chicken breasts

It's hot and sticky in Atlanta from June to October. I love making really beautiful composed salads for dinner. This recipe is what I would do, but of course, with all my recipes, add or subtract whatever you want. Obviously you're not going to feed a crowd with a composed salad, but for a small dinner party of four or a night at home with your partner, this is a perfect plate.

DIRECTIONS

1. Prepare all the salad ingredients ahead of time. Eggs and beets need to be fully cooled before you compose the salad. For the beets – cut in quarters and steam them in a pot. After they are cooked, put them in cold water with some ice to cool rapidly. You should be able to get the skin off by working the beets with your fingers. Or if you can't, use a paring knife.

2. Arrange the salad on a plate. I start with the butter lettuce, torn just a bit and make a small mound in the center of the plate. Then I begin to make wedges around the outside of the plate with all the other ingredients. The beets and tomatoes should be opposite each other on the plate. Cucumber and eggs can make up the other "wedges." Save green onions and gorgonzola for sprinkling over the top of the plate. Place all the plates in the refrigerator while you cook the protein.

3. Grill steak to desired temperature. Or if you're using chicken breast, be sure internal temperature is 165. Slice steak or chicken and place over the top of the salad, overlapping each piece. Sprinkle with cheese and onions and you're ready to serve with MetroFresh Basil Vinaigrette.

PEPPERY FLANK STEAK WITH MINT CHIMICHURRI

SERVINGS

Serves 4

This dinner entrée is perfect for an al fresco dinner in spring and fall. Or, chilled, can be served as the protein at a picnic for a summertime outdoor concert. Serve with a light field green salad and the Red Quinoa Salad, and you'll have a great meal. I also love a fresh tomato caprese salad with this steak.

INGREDIENTS

3-4lbs flank
streak – fat trimmed

Course ground pepper

Kosher salt

1 cup (or so) fresh mint

2-3 cloves garlic (more if
you like a garlicy sauce)

¼ cup fresh lime juice

¾ cup extra virgin olive oil

DIRECTIONS

1. FOR CHIMICHURRI: In food processor, chop garlic and mint. Drizzle in lime juice and EVOO. Salt to taste. Consistency should be that of a loose pesto. It should be slightly salty and tangy. Can be stored in sealed container for up to a week.

2. Coat flank steak with a little salt and course ground pepper. Steak can be grilled to completion (to desired temp) or seared in large skillet and broiled in 425 oven – about 15 minutes until internal temperature is 140 degrees.

3. Slice steak very thin and arrange on platter. Spoon chimichurri over meat or serve separately. Steak can be served hot or chilled and served cold.

OTHER MEAT OPTIONS: London broil or sirloin steak, lollipop lamb chops or roast lamb.

EVERY DAY SPICY TURKEY MEATLOAF

SERVINGS

Serves 6

INGREDIENTS

1lb ground turkey

1 package hot Italian turkey sausage, casings removed

1 medium diced red onion

½ cup diced red pepper

½ cup diced yellow pepper

2 eggs

½ cup chopped parsley

2 TBS Worcestershire

½ cup ketchup

2 cups panko bread crumbs

White cheddar cheese (optional)

Salt and pepper to taste

Richie and I have a go-to "random Tuesday" dinner. I'll get a call or text any weekday about 3pm: *Turkey meatloaf?* It usually means Richie and Winnie, his assistant of 30 years at The Richie Arpino Salon, have a busy schedule the next day, and if I make my "famous" turkey meatloaf, they'll be in lunch heaven with leftovers from our table, while they trim, cut, dye and foil all of Atlanta's finest! Here's the recipe.

DIRECTIONS

1. Preheat oven to 375.

2. Using your hands, work together turkey, sausage, onions, peppers, parsley, Worcester sauce, ketchup, and eggs. Pour in panko breadcrumbs and mix until all breadcrumbs are fully integrated into the meat. For best results in cooking, place meat mixture on a cookie sheet and form a 4-in. wide "loaf." It'll be about 3 inches high and 10-12 inches long.

3. Insert 6 pieces of cheddar cheese into the middle of the loaf at about 2 inch intervals (cheese is optional, but we love it!).

4. Drizzle ketchup over the top in an argyle pattern. Bake in preheated oven for about an hour, or until instant read thermometer reaches at least 165 when inserted into the center of the loaf. Important! Do not undercook ground meat!

5. Serve immediately with steamed broccoli and a baked sweet potato! YUM.

THAI COCONUT AND SWEET CHILI STIR FRY WITH SEARED SALMON

SERVINGS

Serves 2

INGREDIENTS

Two 6-8oz portions
skinless salmon

¼ cup canola or olive oil

¼ cup julienne red onion

½ red pepper, julienned

½ cup chopped
oyster mushrooms

1 small handful (about ½ cup)
snap peas, stems removed

2-3 minced garlic cloves

1 "knuckle" minced ginger

1 teaspoon chopped lemon
grass (optional)

½ of a small yellow
squash, diced

½ of a small zucchini, diced

2 TBS low sodium soy sauce (more
or less according to taste); for a GF
dinner, can be omitted

Juice from 1 lime

½ cup sweet chili sauce

3/4 cup light coconut milk

½ bunch roughly
chopped cilantro

Sliced avocado and mango
(Optional)

Baby spinach

White or brown rice

This is another great "Random Tuesday" meal at our house. This meal is extremely easy to prepare and there is a huge margin of error. The ingredients, especially the vegetables below, are what I use, but feel free to add or subtract as you wish.

DIRECTIONS

1. Heat oil in a large skillet or shallow wok over medium high heat. Gently place fish, top side down, in the center of the pan. Cook for about 3 minutes and flip. Cook for another 2-3 minutes to sear the underside. Remove from skillet and set aside. Do not cook fish all the way through.

2. Toss in onion, mushrooms, squash, and snap peas and stir fry for a couple minutes. Add ginger, lemon grass, and garlic and continue to fry, either shaking the pan or using a wooden spoon to move vegetables around.

3. Add soy sauce and squeeze lime juice. Cook for another minute or until vegetables are just tender (I like my veggies al dente, but you can cook them until desired tenderness). Place fish back in the bottom of the skillet and turn heat down to medium. Add cilantro. Drizzle sweet chili sauce and coconut milk over the whole skillet and stir once to mix. Simmer for another minute or two until fish is just cooked through.

4. Remove fish and place on a small bed of baby spinach or rice. Portion stir fry over the fish in each bowl and pour remaining juice. Top with sliced avocado and mango if desired. Serve immediately.

WINE AND LIME POACHED FISH WITH WARM FAVA BEAN OR ENGLISH PEA AND TOMATO SALAD

SERVINGS

Serves 2

INGREDIENTS

2 6-8oz. fish of your choice – white fish works best

2 medium sized shallots, diced.

2 TBS blended canola/olive oil or canola oil (use a light oil for this process, don't use EVOO as it is a little too strong)

1 cup of white wine – chardonnay works great, but you may also use a sauvignon blanc or pinot grigio (Really, whatever you have hanging around your fridge)

¼ cup fresh lime juice

1 TBS Dijon mustard

Kosher salt

This recipe is SO easy you won't believe it. It's almost foolproof and the best thing is, you can make it at home and your kitchen won't smell like fish for a week.

Choose any kind of light, flakey fish you like. Salmon works well and is usually readily available at Publix or Kroger. But if you want something a little more delicate (and are willing to spend just a little more money) go to Whole Foods and splurge. Halibut is perfect when it's "running" but I also like using sea bass, flounder, sole, trout, or tilapia. The cooking method works well with both thick and thin cuts — you'll just adjust the cooking time depending on how thick the fish is.

You'll need a skillet with a lid that fits rather tightly.

Note — if your choice of fish has skin, you can either have the fishmonger remove it for you or poach with skin side down. When fish is done, you can slide a spatula between the meat and the skin and it should come off easily. Discard the skin before serving.

DIRECTIONS

1. Heat a small amount of blended oil in the bottom of a medium size skillet over medium high heat. You'll want the oil to be hot but not smoking.

2. Add shallots and sauté for 30 seconds or so. Don't let the shallot caramelize – you want it to be almost raw.

3. Pour in about a cup white wine. Depending on the size of your skillet you may need a little more or a little less wine – it's not an exact measurement. You want the wine to be about ½ an inch on the bottom of the pan and bring to a boil.

4. Lightly salt both sides of the fish and place in center of the pan. Immediately pour about ¼ cup of lime juice over the fish and cover. Turn heat down to medium and continue to cook for 5-7 minutes, depending on the thickness of the fish. Fish is done when it can be flaked with a fork.

(CONTINUED)

FOR THE ENGLISH PEA AND GRAPE TOMATO SALAD

About 1 cup blanched fava beans or English peas (use the peas when they are in season in spring. You can also use edamame!)

1 cup or so halved grape tomatoes

2 TBS extra virgin olive oil

Kosher salt

Fresh basil

1. While fish is cooking, toss peas and tomatoes in small bowl and coat with a little olive oil and a pinch of salt. Heat a tablespoon of olive oil in a small skillet over medium high heat. Pour in the salad mixture and toss a few times until just heated through but not really cooked. Remove from burner and toss in a pinch of chopped fresh basil.

2. By this time your fish should be perfectly cooked. Place fish on the bottom of a large shallow pasta bowl. Stir Dijon mustard into the liquid that remains in the pan and cook for another minute or two. Pour poaching liquid over the top of the fish and scrape any remaining shallots from the bottom of the pan.

3. Spoon warm salad over the top. Garnish with a small amount of daikon (radish) sprouts or a sprig of parsley and serve immediately.

Thought

Subscribe to our
daily menu

enter email address

MetroFresh MIDTOWN

JUMP TO TODAY'S MENU

LOCATION / HOURS / TEL

Go to...

MENU-
THE FOOD
BREAKFAST
CHEF BIOS
PHOTOS
RECOGNITION
UPCOMING EVENTS

Friday, July 10, 2015

hello, metrofreshuals!

by Mitchell

After coming clean on last week's movie adventure, you know, the one that rhymed with Nifty Maids of Hey? I'm loathe to admit this new adventure. Nevertheless, I'll come clean, as I am want to do. Last night was date night. We haven't had one in a while, so it was high time we had a dinner and a movie evening with just the two of us. Naturally, this included an amazing Tio Miguel dinner here at MetroFresh of Eggplant Parmesan for Richie and Roast Duck with Orange Sauce for me. OMG, it was good! Then it was on to Midtown "Art" Cinema for a movie. I put "Art" in what I wish were air quotes because while our movie choice was highly entertaining, there wasn't anything that closely resembled art in it.

Yes, you've probably surmised by my typically circumspect writing that last night's epic celluloid experience rhymes with Tragic Tike. Ok, I'm just going to go ahead and say it. Richie and I were the only men in the theatre. Well, maybe there were two more, but basically, if there ever was a chick flick, this was it. In terms of a review, well, there's not much to say. It was highly entertaining, but completely devoid of conflict. And of course, there was lots of skin and pelvic thrusts. My heavens, it even made *me* blush. But you know what? News these days is pretty depressing – all serious and completely full of conflict. Maybe the best thing to do is have 123 minutes in a nicely cooled movie theatre, in the dark, to just have fun and not worry about the world quite so much. Yes, that's what entertainment is for. And if it were not for the four rather depressing trailers for coming attractions, the entire evening, from Duck to Popcorn, would have been completely drama free. And that's what date night is all about.

It's Friday, my friends, so we're doing tacos! Lobster, roasted Pork and Grouper! Each order comes with three of one or you can get one of each. And because it's a lot food, and so delicious, we don't offer a free side with it. Instead, if you'd like a side, just add $3. Have a great Friday!

Let us bring the MetroFresh experience to your next event.

SUNDAY BRUNCH @ M
EVERY SUNDAY 10-3

eat breakfast at metrofresh!

THOUGHT

When I conceived of this book, I decided to call it FOOD&THOUGHT since the story naturally includes food, but also, this crazy collection of thoughts I've managed to stockpile over the last ten years.

MetroFresh opened on Monday, October 10, 2005. My menu changed every day and I had this idea to get it to potential customers via their email. I wanted customers to be reminded of this new restaurant when they sat at their office desks or kitchen tables and opened their computers each day. I thought they might be tempted to come in and buy something! If you can believe it, social media didn't exist then. So email was the only (and cheapest) way to get information to customers "a la minute," as they say in the kitchen. It was, by today's Facebook, Twitter, Instagram standards, pretty primitive.

The first task was getting the menu in as many in-boxes as possible. The next task was getting as many potential customers to open that email as possible. I thought if I could get them to "buy into" this new restaurant on a personal level they'd become frequent guests. So I decided to include a personal note from me.

At first the stories were mostly about the restaurant—"The Adventures in Restaurant World." And then I began incorporating stories about my life—from home with my partner Richie, from family past and present, from the world around us. It was a way to tell the story, to continue my life as a communicator.

The first year and a half, I used Outlook with email groups. See what I mean—almost prehistoric! Sadly, I didn't save any of those early emails. And then in 2007 we got all sophisticated with a new email marketing program called Constant Contact. It was a life-changer. It sent emails to a couple thousand people with a single click of the mouse. And, more importantly for me, the emails were saved automatically.

What follows is a compilation of years and years of daily stories. Most people now call this kind of thing a blog, but I'll always call it "The email."

I have spent six months collecting, cataloging, and editing my emails. They read like a stream-of-consciousness journal, telling the story of the last decade with all its highs and lows, its triumphs and tragedies, its sacred and profane. Because there are so many to catalogue, I had to arbitrarily have a cutoff date, which was somewhere around the middle of 2014. The good news, is that there are lots more, written every day, so who knows? Maybe there'll be a second volume one day!

Writing daily is a challenge. Had I set out to "write every single day no matter what!" I never would have done it. But day after day, as the months and years have gone on, I have found a comfort in the discipline of my morning chore. Naturally some days are perfunctory—just the facts ma'am sort of thing. These are usually days when the business of running a busy restaurant really doesn't allow and even an extra ten minutes at the computer. But more often than not I have been able to come up with something that strikes me, whether it was something that happened last night at home, a funny thing I heard on the news, an event at MetroFresh, or a memory from my childhood.

In the end, the journey is the destination. I wonder who originally said that? I believe it to be true. My life's journey has been incredible. I'm beyond grateful I have been able to share the journey with a devoted partner, a loving family, and in the last ten years, a new family of MetroFreshuals—actual and virtual.

The pages that follow will not stop the earth from rotating. They won't silence the guns or heal the sick. They don't contain the profound thoughts of a Maya Angelou, the humor of a David Sedaris, or the philosophy a Deepak Chopra. These pages are just me and the story of a somewhat co-dependent, hardworking, sleep deprived, chef/owner of a little restaurant in Midtown Atlanta, with a big mouth!

Enjoy…

SATURDAY MAY 5, 2007

It is both Derby Day and Cinco de Mayo and I have neither bonnet nor sombrero. Poor me.

SUNDAY JUNE 17, 2007

Happy Father's Day!
A few words of wisdom from my father, R. Quintus Anderson.

1. The best part of the day is between 5am and 7am. After that, you might as well go back to bed!

2. The turtle only gets ahead by sticking his neck out.

3. When you graduate from college, you are welcome to come and visit any time. But you are now responsible to make your own home, and you are not welcome to live here!

4. If you need to chew gum, do it in your closet.

5. Wake up every morning and ask what you can do for those around you.

6. Remember that decisions are hard—but also remember that the most important thing is to MAKE a decision, and then go for it.

7. If you are not fifteen minutes early, you are late!

8. Have fun. Give generously. Be kind.

I honestly try to live by most of these. My father is a kind, generous, smart, and gentle man. He was very successful in his life and taught us the most important thing you can do is share success with others. We would not have a MetroFresh if it were not for his support, guidance and encouragement.

When I began this journey into owning my own business, I had come from the flaky world of the arts. My father had always supported my decision to act—he was always proud of my accomplishments on stage and screen. But when I changed direction and headed into the business world, suddenly we could speak the same language! I feel like this new journey has led me closer to him and for that I am immensely grateful. Now if I could just learn to like golf!

I love you, Dad

Dad at Andover 1949

WEDNESDAY NOVEMBER 21, 2007

Today I get to do my third annual "What I Am Thankful for—What I'm Not Thankful for" list. So here goes:

1. I am thankful for Richie and Elmo and my home. Life is worth living because of them. I am not thankful that they both snore—no kidding!

2. I am thankful for Rockstar and his talents in the kitchen. He is a tremendous asset to MetroFresh. I am not thankful for the A&R record execs, who will eventually discover him and take him away from me!

3. I am thankful for Topher because of his perseverance in adversity, his creativity, and his humor. I am not thankful for the jerks (I would say another word, but you never know who is listening) who broke into his new house and disturbed his peace.

4. I am thankful for my whole staff and their dedication to who we are at MetroFresh. I am not thankful when they can't seem to find ANYTHING in the fridge.

5. I am thankful for my family—Mom, Dad, Brothers and Sisters (not the show, my family, although there are similarities). And for Richie's family, who are my own now for TEN years. I am not thankful (frankly, I'm mad as hell) that our sister-in-law Janie passed away this year from breast cancer.

6. I am thankful for my awesome customers, who have kept us going, entertained us, and energized me for more than two years.

7. I am thankful that I have my health and I can still get up at 4:30am to make soup—except when I am not thankful and I really want to sleep in.

8. I am thankful for Souper Jenny and for our friendship. She continues to teach me so much about life and the kitchen. I am not thankful she can drink me under the table!

9. I am thankful that I know generous and wonderful people, and that there are amazing people in the world that I don't know, doing incredible work for peace, the environment, human rights, health, and poverty I am not thankful that many people don't seem to care.

WEDNESDAY DECEMBER 19, 2007

So here's the thing!

When you are married to a ROCK STAR (Richie, not Bryan), sometimes you have to party like one. Last night was the second annual Eddies Attic "Ed Roland and Friends" fundraiser for Hero for Children. Ed (of Collective Soul, whose CD cover was shot right here at MetroFresh) collected several of his incredibly talented friends to play a couple of songs each for a sold out crowd. The coolest thing is to see Ed share the spotlight with some of Atlanta's finest young talent. What an amazing opportunity for them to play a sold out show at Eddie's Attic with a real Rock Star (Ed, not Richie.)

But talk about a Rock Star—Richie rocked the house! It is amazing that I have been a performer for my entire adult life and I would never have been able to do what Richie does on a regular basis. He loves to sing, to play, and to entertain. He does it all—and he is REALLY GOOD. He held his own with the upstarts and the veterans, and my biggest task today is to get him to go back to his regular life at the salon where he is a ROCK STAR as well. I was so proud of him.

Look for a young guy named Ben Deignan (he has an unpronounceable last name); he was amazing.

Now, I excused myself at the respectably late hour of midnight after reluctantly accepting a shot of Patron from radio personality and general instigator of mirth, Jeff Dauler. Then the rest of them went on to the After Party. I always say, leave them wanting more, so I left. I am not at all sure they cared, but at the time there were large protestations of "What? You're leaving?" ,"You can't go home NOW, the party is just starting" and "All you have to do is make soup—how hard can that be?"

If only they knew.

Truth be told, I was not in the kitchen super early this morning because Rock Star (Bryan, not Richie) was here for the early shift, but I do have a long day ahead prepping for a big party we are doing tomorrow night. It is tough being the responsible one in the family, but I guess that is why they don't call me Rock Star—they call me Poppa.

Richie being a rock star on the MetroFresh Patio

FRIDAY MARCH 28, 2008

It is early Friday morning and, guess what? I am coming home. But more importantly, my Dad is coming home! I am about to leave with a set of clothes, a steamer trunk, and a U-Haul to get him. During a ten day hospital stay one sure collects a lot of stuff.

Dad is definitely on the mend, but he will have 24-hour care for a little while and he will have to use a walker until the knee he injured after his last fall has time to heal. Key to the next month or so is keeping him on his feet. We really cannot make ANY return trips to the hospital any time soon! My days down here for the last week have been longer and harder than my days at MetroFresh. I am ready to get back in the kitchen and take a break! I know Rockstar will be happy that I am getting back.

So I hear Topher was looking for "Things I Wish I Had Learned in High School." I thought I would add a few from my experience this week—because high school doesn't prepare you for what we have been through this last month with my parents:

Dad at his 80th Birthday, 2010

1. **Learn humility**—When you are helping your father from bed to chair while he is wearing a hospital gown, there is no room for pride.

2. **Learn to manage time**— Shuttling between the hospital and the house, Publix and the pharmacy, all while trying never to leave either parent's side, causes quite a lot of stress!

3. **Learn geography**—Because if you have to spend a week with your parents in Florida during their later years, you may not really know the ocean is even there.

4. Learn to be bossy with a smile —Well-timed boss-iness can, if you are polite yet firm, get things done. Especially with overworked nurses who are working on twenty more pressing things than your parent's need for a new pillow. But your parent still needs that pillow.

5. Learn to be patient —Because you are going to need a whole lot of it when you get to this stage of your life. You have to deal with a lot of people who will work your last nerve. But slamming down the phone or raising your voice is not going to get you any further ahead.

6. With apologies to Elton John —learn to respect the "Circle of Life." It really is amazing how we grow into middle age and become the care givers of the people that cared for us. This is the journey and the poetry of life: to have parents who loved uncondi-tionally and to have the time and honor to return that love unconditionally. It takes all the lessons learned above, but without this step on the path, those other lessons wouldn't count as much.

Dad at his 80th Birthday, 2010

SUNDAY MAY 11, 2008

So today is Mother's day. It was pouring this morning when I came to work, but the sun seems to be coming out. The patio will be clean and dry for a lovely lunch with the most important woman in your life.

Things I learned from my mother:

1. **Always make your bed.** You never know who might visit!

2. **Competition is good,** play to win, but play with grace and an eye on your personal best. Beating the other guy isn't as important as the satisfaction that you did your best.

3. **Always give to others.** Time, money, energy, and spirit are commodities we all have in endless supply (maybe not the money part), but if you give, you will always find happiness and it will come back tenfold.

4. **Discover your true self and be proud of that person.** If you stay in your truth, you cannot fail.

5. **Be creative with your life.** Find beauty and joy in the mundane and your life will never be boring.

6. **Write thank-you notes.** And stuff the envelope with the salutation facing out!

7. **Never wear a hat indoors.** This is rule number one. The surest way to get on Mom's bad side is to keep your hat on in the house.

8. **Stand up when someone comes to your table,** or when a lady enters a room.

9. **Never sit at the dinner table before Mom** - and don't forget to pull her chair out for her.

10. **Go the extra mile** - at work, at play, with family and friends.

With Brooks and Mom at Brook's high school graduation.

These days Mom's doesn't have the energy she had when she was young with six kids, serving on the school board, President of the WCA Hospital, owning her own business, and teaching us to be kind and polite (see above.) But when you ask her how she is doing—after all she has gone through with her health over the last few years, she always says, "Oh, I'm just fine." I know this is a lie, she hates sitting in a chair, she resents ringing the bell when she needs help, she misses playing golf something awful—but Mom taught us to be happy and to live life. I love my mom for every time she sat in some sweaty pool natatorium to watch me swim, for every cast party we had when she decorated the house, for sitting through every play, concert, and recital. For being a really good mother!

Happy Mother's Day, Mom—I love you!

THURSDAY AUGUST 7, 2008

Yesterday was just one of those days. I had 1.5 million things to do—staff meeting, catering proposals, manager stuff, and dinner at MetroFresh. In midst of it all, I kept getting phone calls from Richie.

Call number one: "Can you meet me at the Humane Society?" "Uh, no, I am kinda busy just now."

Call number two: "I am at the kennel and there is another family looking at THE DOG." "Well, if it's not meant to be, then it's not meant to be."

Call number three: "Paleeeeease can't I get her? I promise to take care of her." "You're an adult, you can make this decision, but remember, I am currently working 50-60 hours a week. You will have to do the lion's share of the puppy training."

I wait. Uh-oh, no call number four.

So I'm m here in the steaming hot MetroFresh kitchen, frantically trying to pull dinner together after the staff meeting. I have three orders of lamb sliders (which were delicious by the way) on the grill and a piece of salmon in the frying pan, and I happen to look out the door. There he is, Richie, holding the world's cutest black puppy. I didn't even have time to run out and kiss the new arrival on her little black snout. But, just as I predicted, by 5:30pm yesterday we were new parents.

Here are the vital details. Her name is Schotzi, which we learned is the German word for what you call your sweetheart. She is a lab/chow mix, or something along those lines, and she is completely midnight black. Elmo seems pretty okay with her so far. Schotzi just wants to play. And she is ADORABLE!

Everyone who wrote back about yesterday's email encouraged me to green light the puppy. Normally I am not the "stick in the mud" kind of person. So with quiet acceptance, I went along with a new addition to the Anderpino family. And puppy makes four in Morningside! I haven't had a dog for 14 years; my last was named Caliban, and he was an amazing animal. So I am pretty confident that with all the love in our house,

Schotzi has a good chance as well. And I promise to spare you the details of puppy's first successful housetraining or puppy's inevitable destruction of the furniture.

Schotzi's first day at home, Summer 2008

THURSDAY AUGUST 21, 2008

So here is the thing about birthdays—you can't believe that the number after your name keeps getting SO big. Today I enter my late 40s. It seems pretty impossible that I am THAT old, and given the fact that most of the people I work with on a daily basis could be my adult children, I alternate between feeling my age and not believing my age is even possible. Those creaky feelings in my muscles and joints are daily reminders that, in fact, I AM that old. But my association with this very young crew every day reminds me that I have more in common with them than I do with, say, Senator Obama, who is both a Senator and running for President and is also just a week older than me! No doubt he has more gravitas than I do (he certainly is a lot smarter) but I bet you can't Youtube an old episode of 21 JUMP STREET and find him!

At any rate, I do feel as though my life has been lived well. I have done a lot of things, made a pretty good living in two careers for which I feel great passion, made and kept friends all over the country and created a home life I wouldn't trade for Bill Gates' bank account. When you are younger (like my staff), you have to run around and experience life. For some reason this happens mostly late at night. You show up for work as though you were ridden hard and put away wet. When you are almost a half century old, you can lie on the couch, watch the Olympics with your fat cat, your rambunctious puppy,

That's me, looking sweet in about 1967

and your loving partner and be completely happy! This is the grace that comes with age. Yippee!

All I want for my birthday is to help Soledad pay her daughter's medical bills. If you are so inclinwhen you come in, drop a dollar or two in the jar next to the cookies. Thanks to our amazingly generous customers we have raised over $500 in just two days. We will know more of her condition after she sees a specialist tomorrow. I just know this is all going to cost a lot, but with your help, she can worry not about paying the doctor, but her daughter's health. Thank you again.

THURSDAY SEPTEMBER 11, 2008

Having played the role of Nurse Betty to the recovering Richie Arpino, who underwent a minor surgery, I would like to give you some tips when you have to wear the nurse's cap for your loved one.

1. Have patience for the patient. They will think that the pain will NEVER go away. Gently remind them that it will. Then double up on the pain meds!

2. Don't ask "can I get you something?" more than, say, once and hour—its super annoying to your patient, and they will most likely bite your head off and forget you are only trying to help.

3. While Nurse Betty is sure she is ALWAYS right, she shouldn't push her luck—if you know what I mean.

4. Screen all incoming calls from well-wishers. Having doubled up on pain meds, the patient is in no condition to accept calls. And by no means allow visitors in the first 72 hours (see below).

5. The third morning is the worst. Then, like a miracle (and a double dose of pain meds) the corner is turned. Light can be seen at the end of the tunnel. Not the "head towards the light" light you think you are seeing after surgery, but the very real possibility of light at the end of the tunnel.

So we have turned the corner. Richie is doing much better and has been a great sport, but, seriously, they ought to tell you it is okay to take two pills.

THURSDAY OCTOBER 11, 2008

Happy Birthday to Us!

When we started this journey of MetroFresh on October 10, 2005, I knew it would work. I had nothing to base that ridiculous over-confidence on except that I was raised by incredible parents who gave me the life skills, education, manners, and temperament to think I could do just about anything. After all—I had gone into the incredibly stable world of Show Business for twenty years and that worked out pretty well, why not have a second career in the ultra-stable restaurant business. Seriously—was I crazy to think I could do this? My education and my confidence was a direct result of good parenting, my blind fearlessness was the result of some kind of blind naiveté. But I chose good teachers, most especially Souper Jenny, who gave of her time, talent, and humor to introduce me to this new world. I had always known, but was reinforced by her, that food is means to bring together people. Community! My former chosen career did that too, if you take out all the bull crap.

So now we have achieved something we all can be proud of—whether you're behind the counter, in the kitchen, or as you continue to walk through the door. MetroFresh has been my life quite a long time now. With the incredible support and love I have received from my number one supporter, Richie; my amazing friend and mentor, Souper Jenny; my incredibly dedicated and hilarious staff in front of the house; and the talented and hardworking kitchen assistance of Soledad, Yukari,

Maya, Sonia, Tio Miguel and, especially Rockstar, we have been around long enough to witness life.

We have fed children-to-be in-utero, seen them as babies wearing mini-MetroFreshaul bibs eating their first solid food—usually chicken barley soup, and witnessed first steps and first words. We have been part of incredible weight loss and promises to eat healthy, whole food. We have said good bye to MetroFreshuals who have moved to different parts of the country and around the world (many of whom still read these emails) and said hello to new neighbors and friends. We have helped nourish people when they were sick and watch them return to health. And, sadly, we have watched as our friends and family pass from us.

Today as we celebrate our entrance into our fourth year, we celebrate life in all its stages. We chose to honor the memory of Lisa Farmer because in so many ways, she represented who we are as a company. Lisa walked in here in the first week and took us on as her cause. She was no longer practicing law because of her fight with MS, but she had the fire of a mother, wife, and VA/Highland crusader, who gets behind a project and then there is no stopping her. Lisa brought Chris and Brian (her husband and son) many times a week that first year—giving advice, praise, and criticism in equal doses. She always gave it with the great knowledge that all MetroFrehsuals have a stake and "ownership" in who we are and what we put out to the world. Brian was only two then, but we watched him grow into an amazing young boy who is kind, giving and, with a touch of his mother.

Lisa, Chris, and Brian Farmer

Then, sadly, we got the news that Lisa had one more roadblock in her life. She passed away a few weeks ago and reinforced that life, in all of its joys and sorrows, happens all around us at MetroFresh. We are grateful to be part of that circle in a community that cares about us and each other. We invite you to share in our accomplishment of making it three whole years. If you are able, give a donation in Lisa's honor to the National MS Society.

SATURDAY OCTOBER 18, 2008

So yesterday, as many of you may have noticed, we got some very much needed rain. I, and most of the people I know, heard a weather forecast and were anticipating the "rain event." Unfortunately, Richie didn't get the memo so he thought he would continue his gas saving ways and ride the scooter to work at The Richie Arpino Salon in Buckhead. Normally, this is a pleasant ride through the back streets between Morningside and Buckhead. So when the rain started yesterday and didn't stop ALL

day, he was kinda stuck. I offered to go pick him up, but he couldn't leave the scooter unattended in the Friday night craziness up there. So, about 5:30 I went outside to walk the dog, and there he was, turning the scooter into the driveway looking like a drowned hairdressing rat, dripping wet with his black Richie Arpino Salon smock stuck to his drenched clothes. He was wearing a helmet (safety first), but the thing that made the whole look just this side of hysterical were his light blue oversized sunglass which would have benefitted greatly had they been equipped with mini windshield wipers!

Fortunately, Richie has a sense of humor and is not lacking in the ability to see absurdity in his own predicament (much like Lucille Ball). We had a good laugh and he rushed in to peel away his wet clothes and hop into a steaming shower. Plans for drink with a colleague were cancelled, and we had a lovely evening at home with a couple of adult beverages and some of Tio Miguel's Pasta Bolognese from MetroFresh.

Richie's Toy!

WEDNESDAY OCTOBER 22, 2008

Sheer joy is a pleasure to observe, especially when it is exhibited in your loved one. Yesterday, Richie, who has been busy squirreling away his pennies, bought the Mac Daddy of digital cameras. As some of you may know, in addition to being one of Atlanta's favorite hairstylists he has become quite an accomplished photographer. One day, about six years ago, he woke up and decided to start shooting. With years of experience doing hair and make-up on photo shoots, he thought, hell, I can do that! No fear, no second guessing, he just jumped in head first. It was totally inspiring to watch and, if truth be told, gave me the confidence to jump head first into a new field myself. So now, six years and four cameras later, he is still like a kid in a candy store. With a huge fashion shoot for PIEDMONT REVIEW pending, he decided it was time to "upgrade." To me, it wasn't that long ago that we upgraded to the last camera, but to him, this was an opportunity to take the next step.

When I got home yesterday, the kitchen counter had disappeared under the paraphernalia and boxes of his new love; this, the product of a Gemini with no desire to distract himself with things like cleaning while he examines all the nooks and crannies of his new purchase. Later, when he walked in the door at 8:15pm, he was like an eight-year-old with a new bike. Flushed with great work and excited by the pictures, he poured himself an adult beverage and worked at his computer straight through dinner and well after my bedtime.

Here's the thing. Richie has a capacity to experience joy more than the rest of us. In the rare moment I may feel stress at work, or have my eyes pop out when I see my produce bill, or worry about the state of the economy, looking into Richie's world always rights my ship. How lucky am I?

When you come in, take a look at Richie's 2009 Swimsuit Desk Calendar. They are on sale here for $20—all profits from the calendar go to breast cancer charities. I assure you, joy is infectious. And we all need a little right now.

TUESDAY FEBRUARY 24, 2009

So today is FAT TUESDAY! Much revelry and party-ing will go down tonight in many parts of the world, especially New Orleans. So we are going to honor the day with our own Fat Tuesday celebration.

First of all, Poppa (me) is cooking up some shrimp creole with crispy fried okra. It will be my own version of the traditional dish, AND we are having our first "Shrove Tuesday" pancake supper. Pancakes, sausage patties and fruit for just $8. AND children under 12 eat pancakes for free.

Why pancakes? Well, you know we like to bring in food traditions from home; mine happens to be Jamestown, NY. We always had a Shrove Tuesday pancake supper in the church basement. There were no crazy masks or costumes, and aside from the martinis our parents drank before taking us to the dinner, there wasn't much partying, but it was still fun. I never knew why pancakes until this morning when I did a little Googling!

Shrove Tuesday marked the beginning of the 40-day Lenten fasting period when the faithful were forbidden by the church to consume meat, butter, eggs or milk. However, if a family had a store of these foods they all would go bad by the time the fast ended on Easter Sunday. What to do?

Solution: use up the milk, butter and eggs no later than Shrove Tuesday. And so, with the addition of a little flour, the solution quickly presented itself in... pancakes. And lots of 'em.

Today, the Shrove Tuesday pancake tradition lives on throughout Western Europe, the United States, Canada and Australia, but is most associated with the UK, where it is simply known as Pancake Day with a traditional recipe, although these can be as varied in the UK as there are British households.

So there you go. Come to MetroFresh with the kids tonight—you can have a free glass of Sangria with your dinner entrée, kids under 12 can eat free pancakes, and we can all get ready for the dour six weeks to come. We will decide tomorrow what to "give up," but tonight we party. Hey—we'll even have some beads!

MONDAY JUNE 29, 2009

A word about traveling with elderly parents—avoid it at all costs. The trip started fine. We had two care givers, about six thousand pieces of luggage, two cars and me. I found a Jet Blue bag checker who took pity on me, and helped me through the process of identifying bags, ids etc. and we made it to security. I know the TSA tries their best to keep us safe. I know they mean to do their jobs well, but, really, my mother CAN'T walk through the metal detector and the only way they have of checking her for explosives, is padding her down—or more accurately, feeling her up! It was a little hard to watch and everyone in the security area is treated to a free show as they do it in a glass enclosed box. We finally get to the gate after much sweating, having removed most of our clothes, contents of our carry-on bags, the usual stuff, and then the flight kept getting delayed because of a

Mom and Dad on their honeymoon in Bermuda, 1954

"mechanical" problem. Finally, an hour after our scheduled departure they decided to give up on that plane, and give us another, which meant going to another gate. Which, wouldn't you know, in Orlando means going to another concourse and, are you ready? Repeating the security nightmare! I was on the verge of a nervous breakdown. I begged one of the guards for help. He got his supervisor and she took us to the front of the line, thank heavens! But this still meant getting everyone shoes off, unpacking the carry-ons, and feeling mom up AGAIN in the glass house. My siblings awarded me a citation for having the "Most Trouble at the Airport while traveling with Mom and Dad!" Yippee! Finally we arrived in Lakewood exactly 12 hours after we started.

WEDNESDAY JULY 15, 2009

So just like graduation day when your son or daughter goes off to adulthood, we are celebrating today with mixed emotions. Our own Kristin Wright, who was among the first employees at MetroFresh (among the original few, in fact, who created MetroFresh with me), is leaving us today. When we opened MetroFresh, we knew the quality of the people up front, who serve you all every day for many hours at a time, set the tone and created the world we wanted. Kristin has been an integral part of this creation. Most recently, with her love of all things green, she oversaw the transformation of the patio. She has lots of admirers amongst you, and if you are reading this, she would love to see you today. She is on for the lunch shift, so make it in and give her a great big hug.

Kristin's gift of empathy is leading her back to Central America, where she and her friend Mary will "work" for whatever NGO will have them do. And when I say "work" I mostly mean volunteer. They are working to alleviate poverty and suffering of so many people whom they have never met but who will no doubt, in a very short time, be their best friends. I have always hoped the people I hire to represent us in front have a greater ambition. I know, and I want, MetroFresh to be a weigh station on their journey to something larger. I am thrilled that Kristin has found the passion for a life of service (for as long as she does it) and that we were able to give her a home as she figured that out. They call me Poppa around here, and I think one of the reasons is that I encourage my "kids" to find that "thing" that makes them excited to get up in the morning. And like my own father, who encouraged and supported me as an actor and then as a chef/owner of this crazy restaurant, I have nudged Kristin into leaving the safety of a job she has enjoyed to go into a world of great promise, to do great things.

I told Kristin yesterday that when I graduated from college my father said

Kristin Wright, spreading love in Honduras

I was always welcome to come home and visit—he would even pay for it whenever I had the time. But that I was not allowed to come back home to live. So as we send Kristin out into the world, she knows that she can always walk through the door at MetroFresh and she will have a home, but she can't have her job back! She is ready to tackle greater things, and unless MetroFresh becomes a bazillion dollar company and we need a full time horticulturalist, she will have to follow her passions outside the safety of MetroFresh. Richie and I will miss Kristin greatly, but we wish her safe travels, good humor, healthy eating (as I know there is no MetroFresh in Guatamala), and most of all our love. I also happen to know Elmo will miss her the most! All reasons to come in to MetroFresh today!

WEDNESDAY AUGUST 12, 2009

I finally tackled the mess at the corner of our house which looked like an abandoned dump! I had a wheelbarrow full of picks, shovels, rakes, bags, clippers, and gloves. I made it through the scary poison oak, vines, and weeds that are practically hiding the dead tree (which the city of Atlanta won't let us take down.) This particular tree has a crook in it. I got enough of the vines off the tree to peak into the crook and saw something—looked like a book bag. I pulled it out and sure enough, it was a drawstring cloth bag. I was a little scared to look inside—who wouldn't have been? There might have been a rattle snake inside! I gathered my courage and undid the drawstring. Lo and behold, inside the bag were about half a dozen PLAYBOY magazines, circa 1992 (we're talking Anna Nicole Smith) and a bottle of hand cream! I am not kidding! So many questions went through my head. I was confronted with a serious dilemma: what do you do with a find like this? Do you put it back and pretend you never saw it? Do you leave a note and say you should find another spot? Do you just toss it? Do you put it up for sale on EBay? But I still have to wonder, how long had it been there? Where was the hider enjoying his reading material? What will he do when he finds it's gone??? I am sure at some point my newly cleaned yard will be full of toilet paper, or our white house will be egged into oblivion!

At any rate, it is now in the garbage and being picked up today by the Atlanta Sanitation Department. Possibly they will find it and keep the legacy going! Sadly, there is some youngster in my neighborhood who is super mad I decided to clean the mess on the corner!

SATURDAY SEPTEMBER 5, 2009

Ah, Labor Day Weekend—the unofficial end of summer. Back to the grind, back to comfort of a "normal" schedule, the beginning of the rush to the holidays! I won't talk about that, the ever increasing compression of Holloweenthanksgivingchristmas. But I have always loved this time. The lazy days of summer giving way to a new sense of energy, a new sense of purpose, and, like the New Year, gives us an opportunity to restructure, clean out, and start fresh. So in that spirit, MetroFresh has, for the last four years, gotten a bit of a spiff up on Labor Day Weekend. By Tuesday morning we will have had the floors buffed and sealed, the kitchen scrubbed, and the entire restaurant repainted. So we will be closing today at 4pm and reopen Tuesday morning for breakfast at 7am.

Now let me tell you how we used to spend Labor Day. My parents owned a piece of property in the woods in Northern Chautauqua County right near the county seat, Mayville. There was a small clearing in the woods where we had room for tents, a fire pit, and lots of coolers for store brand cola for the kids and Genesee beer for the adults. We called it Camp Mayville and we would go each year with three of our oldest and best family friends. We would spend one night camping: Uncle George was in charge of dinner, Aunt Ginny was the

"nature lady," my dad was in charge of adult beverages, and Aunt Carol was the "nurse." The plan was always to hike to Chautauqua Gorge (a beautiful natural slate gorge) the next morning. We always made it, but it wasn't until I was in high school that I realized that our parents made this hike feeling something like the inside of a cat litter box! Come to find out, the whole Camp Mayville night was one big party in the woods and there was no "camping" involved. I can still remember the sounds of my parents and their friends hooting and howling way into the night as I fell asleep in one of the tents near the fire. Apparently, when I was about five, I was found out of my sleeping bag under the cot, sound asleep. We always begged to stay another night. And it NEVER happened. The 'rents were just too "exhausted" by the revelry and the daytime hike to even consider another five minutes. They needed Monday of Labor Day to recover! I miss Camp Mayville. I miss the dedication with which my

Setting up Camp Mayville for a one night stay

Uncle George cooking up something wonderful!

parents always organized great family gatherings. They made our childhood special by showing us how to love, share, and enjoy not only our own family, but how one's family reaches beyond the walls of the house.

THURSDAY SEPTEMBER 24, 2009

Richie grew up in a little town in mid-Long Island called Farmingdale. It is right next to Massapequa, home to the Baldwins, and was mostly populated by Italian or Jewish families. But there was this one couple who lived next door named Marilyn and George, who were as WASPy as my family. Marilyn and George were more like my parents; they had a cocktail every evening before dinner. To Richie, this was exciting and exotic. To me, this was standard operating procedure. Not so much now, but once in a while, whenever Richie and I decide to have a cocktail at home during the week we always say we are like Marilyn and George. Last night, I mixed up a couple of vodka tonics, and for some reason (perhaps because I had been up since 5am and only eaten a sandwich all day) my Marilyn and George cocktail went straight to my head. And I gotta admit, this morning I am not feeling all that chipper. Not too bad, but I feel a little foggy—like I have some cobwebs in between my ears. Hopefully they will clear because I have LOTS to do today!

SATURDAY OCTOBER 31, 2009

Happy Halloween, everyone! We here at MetroFresh have woken up to a scary day! We have given birth to a ghoulish menu full of dead things and creepy crawlies. As Dr. Frankenstein would say, "It's alive!!!!!!!!" Through alchemy, trickery and a little magic, the menu today is appropriately gruesome—we know you'll enjoy.

HAHAHAHAHAHAHAHAHAHAAAAAAA!

Okay, so enough of that, let me tell you a story about my parents and Halloween at my house. They were, and still are, incredibly creative, generous people. Back in the late 60s in Jamestown, NY, before the dawn of a billion dollar Halloween industry and the only place to get non-flame retardant Batman costumes was the BIG N, which was a low rent discount department store, Halloween was decidedly lo-tech.

But my resourceful and creative parents decided that we needed to decorate our house for the holiday. So dad bought a couple of sheets of plywood and some orange and black paint, and with a couple of quick cuts with a portable jig saw and paint brushes in our hands we created "The Great Pumpkin!" It was an eight foot diameter flat pumpkin, complete with black triangles for the nose, eyes, and mouth and a green stem, and it was a wonder! We propped it up with great engineering skills (my dad was a mechanical engineer at Princeton), completely blocking the front door. We fashioned a PVC pipe that, in theory, was supposed to deliver the candy to various trick-or-treaters through the hole in the Great Pumpkin's

Our Lo Tech Halloween in about 1973

mouth. The whole thing was brightly lit by spotlights and when we put it up, it was basically the best day of the year. When the great pumpkin came out, you knew it was Halloween. Sure, there were some miscalculations on the weight and gravitational pull of a mini snickers not being enough to negotiate the elbowed angles of the PVC pipe coming from my sister's bedroom on the second floor—the candy most of the time got stuck before it dropped in the bag. And sure, the supposedly spooky noises we'd make from the old intercom my mom used to call us up from the basement sounded more like a tin can than a scary movie, but the whole thing was a hit. People from all over Jamestown came to Arlington Avenue to visit The Great Pumpkin. My mother dressed as a witch and sat on a bale of hay next to him, and, even if she didn't exactly scare the kids, she added to the ambience. The six of us would run out and do our

trick-or-treating in about ten minutes so that we could be home in time to fight over whose turn it was to send the candy down the pipe and make spooky noises on the intercom. Turned out, the best delivery system was one of us just standing behind the thing and pushing the candy through the mouth, but it didn't matter. It was The Great Pumpkin and it was pure joy. It was a family thing and it was ours to share with the rest of the town. And I thought that was just swell.

So that was my Halloween for many years as a kid. It never got old until I did, and I still miss that Great Pumpkin. I miss what it stood for in my childhood: that my parents really tried to make our lives fun, that their gift for spreading joy to others was infectious, and that with a little plywood and some PVC pipe, you can create magic!

THURSDAY DECEMBER 31, 2009

Alright, so sayonara to the last decade—thank god and good riddance to you! It was definitely the decade when things changed—no question about it. My most memorable moment of the decade was, like most people in the world, 8:48am on September 11, 2001. I was in New York City watching the TODAY SHOW like any other morning, when suddenly everything changed. Richie was here in Atlanta, slowly waking up, and I tried to describe what had just happened and what I just saw, which made no sense at all. There were no words, except "Oh my god!"

But here's the thing. At the time, I was still pursuing my acting career. I had just turned 40, and, while there is no denying that that day changed how we see each other, how we see the world, and how we feel about our own mortality, the most important thing that came from 9/11 for me was that I realized I needed my family. I needed to have one home. I needed the sense that every day, when I finished work, there was a safe home and a safe person (maybe a couple of pets) to go home to. It was just after that I changed my life. I began the process that moved me away from the "I am definitely going to hear something from my agents *today*, for sure," world I had lived in most of my adult life into the world that I controlled. The world I live in now. And for that I am grateful—that through all the sadness, the violence, the anger, there was incredible love for me to "come home to." And, as it turned out, incredible possibility.

With the love and support of my partner Richie, I was able to find a mentor in Souper Jenny and learn this amazingly artistic and fulfilling approach to preparing food and start a new career (that in spite of the economy and all the twists and turns it has taken has become incredibly successful!) MetroFresh was really born from the tragedy of that lonely day in New York, when I didn't know, when *no one* really knew, what the world was going to bring next. I love my new life in Atlanta. I love that our perseverance and determination pushed us to the end of a decade that, let's face it, kinda sucked! And

there was a whole lot more tragedy than just the senseless violence of that day. We have weathered economic catastrophe, drought, deluge, the fall of Tiger Woods, Octomom, and John and Kate's divorce.

Seriously, through tragedy comes triumph. And it is my sincere belief and hope that the new decade will be full of happiness, progress, and ultimately, peace. Not to mention delicious food and the comfort it brings.

MONDAY JANUARY 18, 2010

I went to my first Bar Mitzvah on Saturday. I don't know how I could have made it to my advanced age never having attended this amazing ritual. I was blown away. Not only because Jake Goldwasser did an incredible job with the reading of the Torah, but also because of what the whole thing meant. I was such a novice that it took me (and Renita, the Goldwasser's housekeeper) about five minutes to organize the prayer book which, as most of you probably know, opens right to left. This is VERY confusing! But, frankly, it wasn't all that important to follow along, because the entire service was in Hebrew and was beautiful and lyrical and I really didn't need to know how the words translated. It was better to let the voice of the Bar Mitzvah lead me through the journey and just sit back and enjoy the "music" of the language.

But the part that was so moving, that I felt privileged to be present for, was the part where Jake's parents looked him in the eye and told him how much of a gift he is to his family and to the world. In the Christian tradition, we don't have a similar thing. Confirmation in the Episcopal Church is probably analogous, but it's not the same. I kept thinking through my tears, it was an amazing thing for a 13-year-old young man to hear his parents' words about how much he meant to them. Surely Jake has a lot of growing still to do; undoubtedly there will be bumps along his path, but what a gift to have the very public acknowledgement of what he has meant to his parents and his community. It was the confirmation that things have gone right, that he has taken life's lessons and thrived, and that the expectation of his family, friends, and congregation are that he will continue to grow into a loving, generous, and kind adult. I guess this is the Mitzvah. It was awesome to be part of it!

Jake Goldwasser with his parents Kenny and Gloria

THURSDAY MARCH 11, 2010

I know it's another dreary day. But there is a difference, however slight, between today's rain and, say, a week ago.

It's not bone chillingly cold!

Could it be spring is finally creeping in? The signs are there if you look carefully enough. The cherry tree in front of our house is just beginning to bloom, the buds are definitely there on the Bradford pears, and the daffodils are sprouting everywhere.

It's the daffodils I love the most. Growing up in western New York, where winter started in October and often didn't end until April, seeing the first daffodil every year was like what I imagine Noah must have felt when the dove brought him the olive branch. It was a sign. It was a portent of things to come. We would soon be able to shed the layers of winter, one sweater at a time, and spring would shoot up all around us. In my adult life, I have lived in temperate climates where seasons melt into one another. If you blink, you never see the transition. It's different this year since we have had a rather remarkable winter. But as a kid in Chautauqua County, New York, spring sprang gradually. The transitions between the seasons were as important as the season itself. My grandmother lived across the lake from us in a big house on lots of land. There was a grassy slope from the potato field at the top of a hill that ran down to Route 17, which in late March or early April was yellow with daffodils. You could pick them all day and not change the color of that hill. It is one of my strongest memories of my grandmother—her handing me kitchen shears and sending me up to the highway to pick bouquets of daffodils for my mom and my teachers (I know, what a teacher's pet). At the advanced age of 48, it is a great joy to remember those early springs and the anticipation they brought. While I was always slightly worried there wouldn't be enough flowers, my Grandma never cared. She knew that even if we picked every last one, they would come back again the following year in even greater numbers. She was awesome that way. It was always about sending the beauty and love out and never keeping it close to home. It was about all about trusting the cycle of nature and all its glory. In north Georgia, the bulbs probably don't produce quite like they do up north since the ground doesn't really freeze. So picking them from your neighbor's yard for distribution in the home and area schools probably isn't the best idea. These

Grandma's House on Chautauqua Lake, "Bellview"

days you'd probably get arrested—best to get daffs from Trader Joes. But today, try to enjoy the rain and notice the incremental changes in the garden and on the trees. Spring is, in fact, just around the corner.

WEDNESDAY MARCH 17, 2010

I'm back from points south. Mom and Dad are hanging in there, although I do have to say that leaving after just two and a half days makes Mitchell feel a little guilty. This is not a new feeling. When I was a child, my grandmother hosted Sunday dinners at her house every other week. They were love letters to great American cooking. She would cook all day—standing rib roast, Yorkshire pudding, creamed pearl onions, fresh green beans and even Baked Alaska. Without fail she would tell us, "Oh you know, it's just catch as catch can!"

Really? Grandpa died in 1968 so Grandma was widowed for many years before she too passed away. She lived by herself in the large family home we loved so much. Those Sunday dinners were pure joy. So when we all piled into the Ford LTD wood paneled station wagon to go home just after the ED SULLIVAN SHOW had started she would stand on the porch and say, "Come back when you can stay longer." There was always this little pit in my stomach as I watched Grandma wave goodbye—I hated leaving her alone.

So yesterday when I said goodbye to dad and he was just sitting at the kitchen table in his ever present navy blue blazer and khaki pants, I felt that same sad pit. I don't have the luxury of making up a schedule that allows for extended stays in Vero Beach. I have to make food for y'all, and mom and dad know that. But at the same time, I can't help feeling just a little sad when I leave. I did put up some delicious lasagna and savory pot pies. I stocked the fridge with milk, OJ, and eggs. And I tidied up a few loose ends like ordering a new phone charger, but still, I hated leaving. Sister Tracy and nephew Addison will be there in a couple of weeks and then I am sure the wonder sibling Kris will be there shortly after, but still—you know? It's just a little hard.

WEDNESDAY APRIL 7, 2010

I write this knowing full well that one reader in particular will email, text, or call in his displeasure just as soon as this email appears in his inbox. It is just too good a story not to share. And I am willing to take the hit for your entertainment. I will omit names to protect the innocent; not that this actually happened or anything. I'm pretty sure it is an urban legend. So here goes!

Sunday was a beautiful day. Easter came in like a gorgeous spring flower. The birds were chirping songs, the kids were hunting eggs, and the adults were sipping cocktails. On Lake Hartwell, on a pontoon party barge called appropriately "The Dago Buy," five well-educated, successful, and otherwise worldly men set sail for a day's romp on the still waters. There they loaded up the coolers, loaded up the dogs, loaded up the suntan lotion, and loaded on the floaties. They apparently, however, forgot to load up an adult to supervise. (A note—say for argument's sake I actually know these people and I'm not saying I do. If I had been there, the adult would have been me. But since I was working at MetroFresh, there WAS no adult supervision though, put together, all five men's ages is well over 200.) So anyway, they take a 6' raft named Big Mable with them for a little pull behind the pontoon boat.

Later in the day, when it was time to come home, they put Mable on the platform on the back of the boat and headed west toward the setting sun. Here's where the story takes a turn, for somehow, it didn't occur to these otherwise successful, handsome, well-connected men—some of them executives in fortune five hundred companies, others respected Atlanta business owners—to somehow lash Mable to the actual boat, thereby preventing her from taking a leap into the waters of Lake Hartwell.

During the evening, well after the guys returned from their lake adventure, the main dude said, "Hey, anyone seen Mable?" Alas, it would not be until the next morning when they could piece together what had become of her. Being untethered as she was, she did, in fact, take flight as they motored into the otherwise peaceful late afternoon sun. But here's the kicker—NO ONE NOTICED! So I guess the moral of the story is—if you go out on the lake on "The Dago Buy" always have adult supervision.

SATURDAY APRIL 24, 2010

On the family drama front—do I have a doozy! My dad's oldest brother, Uncle Paul lives in Boston and sadly was moved to hospice care on Tuesday after a long battle with leukemia. He is in his upper 80's and has had a great life. He's been married to my Aunt Ann Marie for about 162 years, he has two great children and several grand-children. And up until he was diagnosed with leukemia he was the most robust of the Anderson brothers. There were originally six and now there are just three. So my dad decided he wanted to go to Boston to see his big brother one more time. It is a sweet and loving gesture which, because of my father's condition, presents a rather interesting logistical challenge. As you know, Dad lives in Vero Beach, FL with my mom and can't fly by himself anymore. I would ask you to get out your number 2 Faber pencil and white pad so you can follow along with how the 82nd Air Born Anderson Division has worked out this trip.

Heidi went to West Palm Beach from New York City last night where she met dad this morning at 7am after he was driven there by the lovely Helen of the Vero Beach Car Service. Kris drove five hours from Vergennes, VT

From Left to Right – Tim, Paul, Quint (Dad), Frank, Dan

to meet them at Logan airport and check them into the Hilton in Weston, MA where they are to visit Uncle Paul in the hospice. Monday morning Heidi will fly back to NYC when I will board a plane at Hartsfield to fly to Boston. I'm supposed get a quick visit with Uncle Paul and my cousins, board a plane with Dad Monday evening and fly back to West Palm Beach. We will be picked up by Helen and delivered back to my Mom in Vero. I wake up Tuesday morning, wait for mom and dad to arise, probably do a little cooking to put up some meals for them to have in the coming days, and then fly from Melbourne back to Atlanta Tuesday night. Are you with me?

It's what you do. Fortunately we have the means, desire, and, with a little juggling, the time to make this happen. My dad has given us an incredible life and it is time for us to step up to the plate. For him to be able to get to Boston to say goodbye to his oldest brother is nothing short of monumental. As we go into our own middle age it is time for us to take care of those who took care of us. I am lucky enough to come from a family that realizes the value of family. For us to drop everything in a moment and step up to help my dad have a sweet final moment with one of his two surviving brothers is a complete blessing. I look forward to the hustle of Monday, the inevitable fatigue of Tuesday and the satisfaction of Wednesday when I am back in the kitchen at MetroFresh knowing we accomplished an incredible thing. We will witness an important transition in my families' lives. How cool.

THURSDAY APRIL 29, 2010

Those of you who read the email last Saturday know that I was supposed to spend Monday and Tuesday in the air flying to Boston to get my dad, flying him back to Florida, and then flying back to Atlanta. Well, as it happens...

Sunday we received word that it was time for us to get to Long Island to be with Richie's mom, the intrepid Jenny Arpino, as she ends her two year cancer battle—she's fought hard the whole way, but she's tired and it is time to sleep. More on that in a minute.

This created a bit more of a logistical issue, since obviously I had to be in two places at once. The decision was made that I would do my Boston trip as planned, get dad back to West Palm on Monday night, and then meet Richie at LaGuardia Tuesday morning—lots of travel but not bad. It's what you do.

Monday morning, on my way to Hartsfield my sister Kris calls and says she's in the emergency room with Dad, who has fallen out of bed and hurt his neck—a sprain? A pulled muscle? A bruise? I don't know by "wheels up."

By "wheels down", Dad and Kris were at Mass General where they were admitting dad into the Neuro Unit since dad HAD BROKEN HIS NECK! I put it in caps for dramatic effect and, no doubt, it was pretty dramatic. But thankfully, there was no serious spinal cord injury and no arteries were affected. He broke his C-1 vertebrae in four places and will be in an Aspen Collar for the next six to eight months. Obviously, he wasn't going to Florida on Monday night; instead, I sent Kris back to the hotel so she could sleep and I stayed on to make sure Dad was comfortable. I'm glad I did. At 4am, my new best friend Nurse Carrie came and woke me from my restless sleep in my lobby chair because Dad had awoken and was very agitated.

It's moments that count. I was there for my dad to talk to him softly and calm him down in the middle of the dark night in a scary, busy hospital. It was a blessing.

Tuesday I flew to Long Island and met Richie in the house where he was born, and saw Jen. The moment we walked into her bedroom she looked at Richie and said, "What did you do to your hair?" After a very challenging 48 hours with my dad, and the emotional anticipation of seeing Jen in her final days, Richie and I knew, at that moment, that while it is going to be difficult, everything was going to be okay. We were going to be okay. It's the moments that count. We're here until the inevitable happens. No doubt, it's incredibly difficult. But it's also amazing, and sweet, and sad, and joyful. It is all these. And as we continue on this journey we'll be savoring the moments because, in the end, they're the only things that count.

TUESDAY MAY 4, 2010

Okay—I'm back! At least for now. Let me see if I can catch you up on the last week. Dad broke his neck in a Boston area Hilton Garden Inn by falling out of bed while visiting Uncle Paul, who had been taken to Hospice. He was in Mass General for eight days being tended by my sisters as they tried to find the right collar that allowed him to eat but also held his head steady enough to heal his neck. He is weak from his ordeal but well enough that yesterday was moved to a PT rehab. Uncle Paul passed away Sunday night. It is sad but not unexpected. He went peacefully and my cousin Trip reports that Aunt Ann Marie was with him for dinner just 45 minutes before. The end of life is part of life, but it is certainly hard to predict. The sweet irony is that with my dad still recovering from his fall, he won't be able to go back to Florida for a week or so and will be in the Boston area for services early next week.

On the Long Island front—Richie and I spent a week at his family's home where his mom is also being tended by hospice with help from Niguel the care giver, Mathew, Richie and me. It seems as though she has some unfinished business and is holding on for now. She actually seemed a little better by week's end than when we first got there. The literature tells you that sometimes there is a rally the last few days, and I think with her sons in residence, Jen was in the rally phase. In some ways she is as sharp as she ever was. Richie told her he paid her bills and was teasing her about the CC balance on her Visa. She said, "I only have $54 on that card." Sure enough—the balance was exactly $54. She also doesn't seem to be having any trouble hearing. As we waited to be picked up for our ride to the airport, Richie sneezed in the living room. Moments later we heard a voice from the bedroom saying, "God bless you." We made the difficult decision to come back to work for a few days. If nothing happens before then we will be back in Long Island this weekend for Mother's Day, which we had planned all along.

Richie and I want to thank all of you for your kind thoughts and prayers during this difficult time. It is crazy what winds up being served as you go through life. Fortunately we have the resources to deal with the emotional turns of life.

That all being said, I am happy to be back in the kitchen. Rockstar, Tio Miguel, and the rest of the MF staff did an incredible job while I was gone. I will be cooking dinner tonight and then doing a double in the kitchen tomorrow to give Rockstar and Tio Miguel a much deserved one day break. I know Rockstar needs it since he spent his spare time while I was gone moving.

THURSDAY MAY 13, 2010

In case you've been wondering where I've been, I have been stuck in the pages of a true life family saga. It has been a tragic non-fiction epic, which if published, would be dismissed as nothing more that over-hyped fiction. It's been a doozy!

Except for a few hours last Tuesday night and Wednesday morning, when I did managed to work, I have been in four different states. I've seen the Atlantic and the Pacific, the Sierra Nevada Mountains and Boston Harbor, the inside of a morgue and the viewing room of a mortuary. We have been forced to look life and death in the face, find love and hope inside the cavern of sadness and despair, and rediscover the super glue that holds my family together is as strong today as it has always managed to be.

Since I have shared so much over the years, I feel obligated to explain my latest absence, which was sudden, unexpected, sad, and — hopefully, eventually — redemptive.

After just eight hours in the comfort of my MetroFresh/Morningside world, I was informed that my older brother Gerrit, who was living in Lake Tahoe, had died. The news of my brother's death took my breath away. Not necessarily because it was out of the blue — he had battled the demons of addiction for most of his adult life, and we had been expecting this phone call for the last twenty years — but because of its timing. Coming on the heels of everything else we had been living though was simply too much. My family, who had rallied with great energy and enthusiasm for ten exhausting days, taking care of my father, saying good bye to my uncle, and spending sweet hours with my mother-in-law, was just beginning to revisit "normal". I was back in Atlanta, excited to get into the routine of work and home, and the phone rang...

As we always do, my surviving siblings and I switched into crisis mode. We hatched travel plans, worked our cell phones, and dispatched ourselves to various parts of the country. My parents had to be told, my nephews and niece had to be comforted, my brother's very tangled affairs had to be addressed, and the grieving process had to begin. It was too much to handle. For the first few days, there was a cloud over our souls, so thick and heavy it was literally hard to breathe (the Lake Tahoe altitude didn't help).

Gerrit died Tuesday night. I was in Lake Tahoe by 7pm Wednesday. My sister Tracy was there by noon on Thursday. We circled the wagons and made lists. We cried a little and then tried to find room to laugh with Asya, 27, Luke, 16, and Seth, 11. It was hard to ignore the circumstances of my brother's life and death, and yet it was easy to see he produced three amazing, smart, and caring children. He gave them an international up-bringing, he taught them love and kindness. Through it all, he somehow prepared them for the day their father was no longer here. It is going to be hard, but they'll be okay. We'll be there to help. Just knowing his legacy is in the eyes and hearts of these three amazing kids is a blessing and a comfort. His life-long disease, which for most of us was incomprehensible, finally proved fatal. No doubt we have a lot of conflicting emotions to work through, but there was a moment Saturday afternoon when the dark clouds began to give way to little rays of light and the healing began. We had gathered on the shore of the lake for an informal vigil to send Gerrit's soul on its way. Each of us in the circle had a moment to tell how we wanted to hold him in our hearts. Luke, a brave, handsome, and articulate young man surprised us all by reading the AA Serenity Prayer. With full knowledge this is a very long email already I am copying some of

Gerrit with his three children - Asya, Luke and Seth

Three generations of Andersons - Gerrit, Dad and Luke

Luke's remarks below. Nothing I can say puts it quite as well as his 16-year-old son.

In remembrance of Gerrit Quintus Anderson, 12/28/59—5/4/10.

As a final note I would just like to say that we might not have a serious illness as my father did, but none the less we should always remember this prayer, not only to honor Gerrit but because I believe that its message is seen in every aspect of life and we should all strive for serenity, whether or not we obtain it.

God grant me the serenity
to accept the things I cannot change;
courage to change the things I can;
and wisdom to know the difference.

THURSDAY MAY 20, 2010

More sad news to report. Sadly, but ultimately thankfully, Richie's mom passed away last night. She had been suffering so much during the last few weeks that it really was somewhat of a relief for her and us. She will remain with us in our hearts—a force of nature.

Jennie Arpino, who would have celebrated her 89th birthday August 3rd was kind, loving, generous, and most of all hysterically funny! She has kept Richie and Mathew laughing for more than 50 years. She taught them how to love and how to feel. Mathew and Richie are who they are because of her. No doubt, she will be missed but there is comfort in the fact she passed in the home she made since the 50's in Farmingdale, Long Island, where she wanted to be.

I'll be away for a few days, but, as always, you will be in great hands with Rockstar, Tio Miguel, and the rest of my awesome staff. Last night's party went off without a hitch. It was lots of work, but I think my lawyer friends liked it. We had a little extra Thai Mango Shrimp, which is making an appearance on the menu today. Enjoy.

Richie with the hilarious and beautiful Jenny Aprino

WEDNESDAY MAY 26, 2010

Okay, so here's the thing. This month has been one for the record books. I won't rehash the whole thing, but suffice it to say, I hope the next month goes a little smoother and my life settles into the routine I know so well. That being said, last weekend in Long Island was pretty amazing. Through the tears of loss, we were able to witness a wonderful passage of life. Jennie Arpino was out of pain and it was more than a relief to see her almost regal in her peacefulness. As hard as it was to say goodbye, we took great comfort in the love and good wishes of dozens of friends, neighbors, family and even the volunteer fire department, who came to pay their respects. Our cheeks were stained with tears, for sure, but overall Richie, Matthew and I came back last night feeling like we sent her off in style and with love. In the end, it is a good life lived that has nothing but the love of those around you that we should all strive for. Mama Arpino had that and so much more.

SATURDAY MAY 29, 2010

Ah, Memorial Day Weekend—the unofficial start of summer. I was at Blockbuster (I know, it's SO old fashioned) and there was a mother with four young boys, obviously a collection of various and sundry families, picking out movies, candy, and popcorn with great gusto. I turned to her and said, "Summer vacation?" She responded, "Yep—just two more months before they go back to school!"

When I was their age, Memorial Day was a big deal, the highlight of which was a parade in Jamestown, New York, down Prendergast Street right into Lakeview Cemetery. I loved it. Most years I marched with one contingent or another—Cub Scouts, Washington Jr. High School band, (in which I badly played the trumpet), or the Boy's Club. We had three junior high schools in Jamestown—Washington, Jefferson, and Lincoln, very original. And sadly, Washington, where I went, had the worst band in the city. But we plugged away and held our trumpets high right down the parade route even as we entered the revered Lakeview Cemetery. I was always moved when we passed the gates and all we marched to was the sound of one snare drum. It was super dramatic. After that there was a ceremony, repeated every year at Soldier's Circle, Jamestown's version of Arlington in DC. It was all very solemn. In my eighth grade year, I was tapped to recite the Gettysburg Address from a stage in front of the flag adorned graves of fallen soldiers. Miss Vanderwerk, the ancient, stern girl's guidance counselor and Honor Society advisor at my school, drilled the address into my memory. We were not allowed to use notes and we practiced weeks before in her office facing the wall opposite her desk. I enunciated and projected myself into a stupor. Naturally, being the nerdy nerderson I was/am, I ate the whole thing up. And by the time I stood behind that podium I recited the famous speech without a misplaced syllable. It was my first real theatrical experience, and I fully believe it was one of the things that led me into the theatre for twenty years.

After that, my family was usually invited to Jack and Betsy Smith's lake house where we had a great picnic; the parents drank a lot of beer and we piled into their shiny wooden Chris Craft Inboard to water ski for the first time that summer. Chautaqua Lake was usually still FREEZING, but one had to keep up with the Smith boys and didn't dare complain about frozen toes. Honestly, as an adult, during those times when you need to crawl into the comfort of memory, I put myself in that shiny old Chris Craft, with my brothers and sisters and my family's amazing friends and feel the exhilaration of that first dive in the cold water of Chautaqua Lake. There was a lot of love there — we were lucky.

SATURDAY NOVEMBER 27, 2010

Today is my father's 80th birthday. Dad was born on Thanksgiving Day, 1930, and the story goes grandma had the turkey in the oven and then went to the hospital to deliver her fifth boy — named, appropriately Quintus. A few days later, when Grandma and Grandpa brought baby Quint home, his brothers were completely dismayed that he wasn't Chinese. You see, my grandfather had told the boys that every fifth child born in the world was Chinese, so it only made sense their new brother was also going to be Chinese. I think they may have been disappointed because in 1930 in Jamestown, New York a Chinese brother would, no doubt, have been something to brag about in school.

"Before the parade passes by!" Nana with Tracy, Brooks and me, again in hat!

Cecile and Paul with five out of six sons. Charles, the third son, died in 1934 of Rheumatic Fever

TUESDAY DECEMBER 14, 2010

I think we all need a little pep talk! So here it is.

This time of year brings out the best and, sadly, the worst in people. We're stressed about the holidays, we're worried we won't be able to get EVERYTHING done, we're anxious about seeing Uncle Al at Mom and Dad's, we're a little tired of hearing "Holly Jolly Christmas" every time we walk into Publix, and on top of that, we're really cold! Yeah, we get it and we're right there with you.

But in the midst of it all, there are the sweet moments when you find the exact right thing to give your partner, you talk to your cousin in Albuquerque who just had a baby, your next door neighbor moves the wise men ever closer to the nativity on their front lawn, and the toys in the Toys for Tots bins are overflowing! It's two-sided, and it's hard to focus on the one when the noise of the other is overwhelming.

So here's my suggestion. Today, take one moment for yourself and say a quiet prayer to your guiding spirit and ask for patience and overwhelming love. Because the season should be about kindness, not about Brookstone Foot Massagers, or the best parking place in the Midtown Promenade. Maybe we can all slide into the holiday without freaking out this year. I'm going to try, even as the whirling dervishes in the MetroFresh kitchen spin like a child's toy top. We're busy, but we're still smiling.

FRIDAY DECEMBER 24, 2010

Christmas Eve was Grandma's time. Since my dad stayed in Jamestown to work for his father, we were the lucky ones in the Anderson family who got the most Grandma and Grandpa time. They lived in a big old house on the lake and we went over the river and through the woods every Christmas Eve for a traditional Swedish Christmas.

Now, my friends, if you've never had a "traditional Swedish Christmas" then count yourself amongst the lucky. By and large it's made up of food that, on any other day of the year, you'd run from. There were some edible goodies, like a Swedish soft cheese called Bond-ost, some baked bean casserole called bruna bornor, and rice pudding or in Swedish, Risgrynsgröt, for dessert. But getting to those things was a little difficult because you had to negotiate the other "delicacies" of Swedish food. Sill, sort of a pickled herring thing you eat on rye flat bread, is really strong, makes your breath smell for days, and I thought kinda slimy (apparently my cousin Amy still orders it for her Christmas Eve). Korv, my father's favorite, is a rough mystery meat sausage kind of thing that's a little like a hard dog treat. And the most famous and least appetizing of all: Lutafisk, a lye cured cod fish that starts out like hard plastic chips and when reconstituted in scalding milk is, charitably, pungent. Grandma made sure there were tons of presents under her tree and we were always super excited to get that part of the party started. However, the catch was, you had to have a taste of each and everything on the buffet.

So...my brothers and sisters and I competed to see who could get the smallest dab of Lutafisk on their plate which actually qualified as "a portion." My father, who heaped the stuff on his plate like he hadn't eaten in months, was the judge. He said he loved it—but I think he just loved his mother! Anyway, there were more than a few years when our dog got more Korv than we did, or one of us would take their sausage filled napkin to the bathroom for a deposit into the toilet. It was always a source of great laughter, and hating the food was part of the tradition. Grandma was the best sport of all. She didn't like it either, but it was a tradition!

It's been a tough year for both of our families. We come into the holiday season a little bruised, but also, a little stronger knowing with certainty that we pulled through, we found peace, and we have love. I believe remembering the details of the past keeps us grounded in the present and gives us strength to keep going into the future. This Christmas Eve, we'll be enjoying our tradition of Il Localino with Gayle and Giovanni, and we'll open up presents tomorrow morning by the fire

Merry Christmas
Happy New Year

CECILLE AND PAUL ANDERSON

Christmas snow at Bellview

with Schotzi and Elmo and then we'll cook a roast with our good friends. No doubt we'll tell the same stories of Christmas's past and we'll howl with laughter. And when it's all said and done, we'll be ready to go into 2011 with hope and joy, confident that life goes on.

MONDAY JUNE 13, 2011

So y'all know I'm really happy with my life. I'm busy, challenged, and excited each day, and I wake up in the morning ready to tackle whatever comes along. It's a great place to be when you're staring the big Five-O in the face. But last night, as I watched the Tony Awards hosted by my former DOOGIE HOWSER friend Neil Patrick Harris, I have to admit I felt my annual twinge of regret. Ok, maybe not so much regret as a healthy dose of longing. I love the theatre! I always contend that in spite of the fact I left New York City for Hollywood when I was just out of school, and most of my career was in front of a camera, I was a better and more fulfilled actor on stage. I was fortunate enough to do several jobs off-Broadway, one of which was a two character play I performed for almost six months. But I never did an actual Broadway show. And, gosh darnit, there was a time when I was in the game and if I had stuck around New York I could have been on the Broadway stage.

Once a year, I watch the Tonys with a lump in my throat wishing I was there. I never have the same emotional reaction when I watch the Oscars or the Emmys.

It's the Tonys that bring it all up. I think mostly it's because in New York it's about the work. It's about creating a work of art that is informed by and dependent on the conversation an actor has with his audience—every performance, eight times a week. It's an awesome feeling. And frankly, once a year, I do miss it. Now, before you get all "why don't you go back" on me, you have to know this feeling of missing it is ok. It's really all good. I left on my terms when I still loved the work, so I get to experience those feelings in a positive light. Neil did

With Neil Patrick Harris backstage at Hedwig, June 15, 2014

a fantastic job and I can't help it—I was proud of him (like I had anything to do with it). And when Daniel Radcliff and the cast of HOW TO SUCCEED brought the house down with "Brotherhood of Man" I was practically weeping. It's pure joy to me, and there's simply nothing better—regret and all.

WEDNESDAY JUNE 15, 2011

You know, some mornings I have nothing to write about. I sit at the computer and it's like pulling teeth to come up with some news. This morning is not one of them. Today is June 15, 2011, and it was on this day in little Farmingdale, Long Island some XX years ago that a little Italian boy named Richie Arpino was born. I say XX years, because if I told you how old he actually is, you wouldn't believe me and my credibility going forward would be questioned. You'd say, "no way!" And I'd have to come up with his original long form birth certificate to prove it and you know how that goes! I'll just say, yes, it is Richie's birthday today and yes, it is a big(ish) one—somewhere smack in the middle of his fifth decade. And I, for one, am glad he was born. The world cannot have too many Richie's and yet, he is one of a kind. If you've ever seen him pull up to MetroFresh on his light blue Vespa with his Aviators and helmet on, smile beaming for all the world, you'd know what I mean. There's just something special about our Richie and we wish him the most happy birthday possible.

In other news...

We are going to have our first MetroFresh wedding! I received a phone call around 6:30 last night from Rockstar. He announced that he had asked Sarah for her hand in marriage! I'm not kidding. Between me and you, I already knew it was going to happen. He told me right after Christmas he was going to do it and had arranged to get his mother's ring down here for when

Sarah Peters and Bryan "Rockstar" Kraatz announce their engagement

the moment felt right. And low and behold—yesterday was the day. He got down on one knee just after 6pm last night and just popped the question. The first time I met Sarah it was love at first sight. She had come into the kitchen one morning very early on in their relationship to say hi. It was one of those really busy mornings and I didn't have much time to "chat," but after our brief few seconds I felt like I just knew her—and I felt like she and Bryan belonged together. It just felt right. As it happened, we needed another person on staff and I called him that same day to offer her a job at MetroFresh. This was one of those instinctive hiring decisions that actually panned out! She had me at hello! Those of you who regularly enjoy breakfast at MetroFresh or call in for delivery know how awesome she is—she basically has EVERYONE at hello. They make a great couple and I cannot be happier for them. I think they'll get married sometime next year and naturally you'll be in on the plans as they unfold. And in one more bit of news, Bryan has asked me to be his best man! And with that I burst into tears—naturally. What an honor. So all the best wishes in the world to our happy MetroFresh couple. If you come in today be sure to take a look at the rock on Sarah's finger and give a little wave to the Rock in the kitchen.

SATURDAY JUNE 18, 2011

So tomorrow is Father's Day. When you get to be my age (now less than two months from a formidable 50) you start reflecting on the man that shaped you. I have many specific, visceral memories of my dad but one stands out every morning when I'm in the kitchen making food for y'all.

Sunday dinners were a production in my house. Most of the time, Dad had gone to Super Duper (our local grocery store) and bought the biggest, thickest steak he could find. Mom was in charge of the stove, so she sautéed the onions, fried the potatoes, steamed the fresh beets, or boiled the corn just off the field. Dad was in charge of the grill and I was there, right next to him. After working all day in the yard, or cleaning out the garage, or puttering in the basement work shop, he would shower and put on a coat and tie. Out of the six of us, I was the one who wanted to work all day right beside Dad. I really loved the work, but mostly I just loved being with him. And because the others didn't really "enjoy" it, I usually had him to myself. Dad traveled a lot when we were kids and those hours we spent weeding, mowing, raking, or cleaning were precious time when I could be alone with him. When the dinner hour came, I'd be there next to dad at the grill in my little three button navy blue Brooks Brother's sports coat, a perfectly knotted striped tie and button down shirt with my hair slicked back with Brylcreem just like dad. We'd grill that steak to a perfect medium rare and it was heaven.

Happy Father's Day to my dad Quint, and all your dads too! Take a moment to remember the sweet times when you got to be by dad's side, it'll make you feel great!

Hanging with my dad

FRIDAY AUGUST 19, 2011

Ok, so many of you know (since I've been blabbing it for months now) that I am about to turn 50. The actual day is Sunday the 21st when I will join Heather Locklear, George Clooney, Boy George, and the President in the half century club. It's been a crazy week and I've got a lot to do before my "little" party thing that Richie is throwing for me. I've got several friends and a couple family members flying in to help me celebrate, so I'm kind of excited. We'll all be here for dinner tonight, kind of taking over the restaurant at 8. I'm going to show off Tio Miguel's cooking!

It's kind of amazing to me that 50 is a couple of days away. Aside from a few aches after the long MetroFresh days, I really don't feel 50—not that I'd know what that actually feels like. I'm just glad I made it this far. And I did it with so much love and so many blessings around me. To have a good, content life, albeit busy and full, is an amazing accomplishment. I have an awesome home, an amazing partner, great friends—(old and new), and this world of MetroFresh that challenges and inspires me daily. You really can't ask for more.

When I turned forty ten years ago, I was still acting. I had a nice career but I really felt it was time to look for something else. I just couldn't stomach being 50 and still having to audition for work. And here I am, NOT auditioning! The life of an actor is by nature temporal and solitary. You spend way too much time thinking about life since much of your year and most of your "job" is spent finding work. You just sit at home staring at your phone, hoping your agent will call. It's exhausting in a way you can't really describe, especially when you get into your thirties and, god forbid, your forties. My main goal was to find the second thing in life that inspired me as much as theatre. With great thanks to an amazing mentor in Souper Jenny, and the support of my partner Richie and my family, I was able to do what many in my former profession just can't do—I got out. I thank god I have someplace to go every day, I have people who rely on me to be there, and I am part of a community

I'm incredibly proud of. Life is a little more in balance and now the alone time is welcome, not a burden. And here's a little bit of irony for you—I have decided to act again! I am signed on to do a play called NEXT FALL by my very good friend Geoffrey Nauffts in January at Actors Express. Go figure!

WEDNESDAY SEPTEMBER 14, 2011

I have some sad news. Elmo, the world's most awesome tabby cat, died yesterday. I know, I can't believe it either. After his recent surgery to drain the cyst on his chin, he was just never the same. He had been failing since my birthday and, in spite of about four visits to the vets between then and now, he was just through. I kept trying to get out of here yesterday to take him in—I knew something was really wrong. But one thing after another needed my attention and I didn't end up

Big fat loveable Elmo

leaving until 4pm. When I got home, he was gone. Just "sleeping" peacefully (I hope) at the back door. Agh! It was super sad, and telling Richie, who is still in New York, was really difficult. He'll be home today and we'll have another good cry together then laugh about what a great life Elmo had.

Not many people know this, but Elmo came into being 14 years ago when Richie decided I needed a companion in Los Angeles of the four legged furry variety. I had never been a cat person and really didn't know what to make of the little orange fur ball. But, damn, if he wasn't the cutest thing on the planet. At that point Elmo was an outdoor, friend to everyone in the neighborhood kind of cat. He went visiting and sometimes he wouldn't come back for days. At one point we decided Elmo didn't think I was famous enough because he would hang out next door with George DeCaprio (Yes, that's right—Leo's dad.) When I moved east, Elmo came indoors and lived for a while with his brother Hot Rod at the Dakota. Hot Rod was an old man at that point and was not all too sure the little orange guy was cool. Elmo would torment him, but in the end, they slept together on the couch. Then Schotzi came along a few years ago and Elmo got a taste of his own medicine. Schotzi terrorized him for a couple of years, but in the end, Elmo and Schotzi were total buds and they slept on the couch together. Elmo literally never met a stranger. When we sold the condo, the buyer wondered if the chill cat was included in the sale.

I really do try to put this into perspective. Elmo lived a nice long life, had lots of love, liked to be around people, was never really sick (until the last month) and didn't suffer too long (plus I didn't have to make some kind of awful decision by myself). So all in all, it's not too bad. We're just going to miss him. Every time I turn on my phone I get to see his cute little whiskers on my Blackberry screen. Pretty cool.

SATURDAY OCTOBER 1, 2011

Today is October 1, 2011. My Nana Rumsey would have been 110 or 111 today (I'm fuzzy on the details of her birth year since I wasn't around, but I think it was 1900 or 1901). She truly was the first great cook I ever knew. Much of what goes on in my head as I'm creating something for our daily menu, or cooking something at home, came from her; it's her voice up there. It's not like I have a box of old recipes on my counter; she was one of those intuitive cooks that put things together in creative and magical ways. There was always a mystical feel to her flavor combinations—you knew there was something extra, but like any good dish, you just had hints of that something special. She put a dash of horseradish in her coleslaw (which she said gave you a terrible halitosis but she didn't care), she'd add anise to her bolognaise, and she loved fresh dill!

This week I made a fresh raspberry sauce that topped toasted coconut ice cream for the Ford Motor Luncheon, and I thought of her. There was nothing as special as going to Rochester to visit Nana and Grampe and having

Nana in the 50's

her raspberry sauce over ice cream. It's seriously one of the best things in life—fresh, light, and not too sweet. She was a great canner of all the vegetables my grampe grew in his amazing garden. All sorts of wonders came out of that garden, from tomatoes to pole beans, from zucchini to red beets. I learned to eat beets at age four just because I had them from Grampe's garden to Nana's stove in a matter of minutes.

But here's the funny thing: she would create these incredible meals, start to finish, but she was NEVER satisfied. This had too much salt, that was overcooked. Of course, it was never true, it was always perfect, so I don't know if she was fishing for compliments, or she had some other secrets she was withholding, knowing the next time she wanted it even better. This is where our culinary worlds depart from one another. Embarrassingly, I am my own best fan in the kitchen. I may not always hit my mark, but when I do, god knows you'll hear about it—ad nauseum!!! It may be a character flaw I've developed late in life, but some days, I think I'm a genius. But if I am (even in my own mind), most of the credit goes to Nana.

TUESDAY NOVEMBER 29, 2011

Burr! It's totally the best soup weather you can get—I love it!

Last night Richie and I put up our 15th Christmas tree. How cool is that? Once again, we have created the gayest tree in all the land: all blue lights and silver ornaments! But the gayest touch of all is a white and silver sparkling ribbon that cascades down the Noble pine like tiny crystal clear mountain streams all from a gigantic bow on top. It's...well, it's...breathtaking!!! Actually, I was pretty impressed we got the thing up at all. These days, we really have to take the moments when we can. There's a lot going on and I haven't been home all that much. So, yes, it's our 15th Christmas season together and now that the tree is up, I have to admit, I'm getting in the mood. Even though the calendar still says November, the weather and the tree say December. It's nice.

Our Big Gay Christmas Tree!

THURSDAY DECEMBER 8, 2011

I was thinking this morning about Christmas traditions, most notably, the Christmas cards my parents sent each year. They started having children in the 50's and each year they sent a picture of the kids. From 1956 to 1961, there was one more kid in each picture! One year, when dad was feeling particularly flush, I guess, or perhaps when mom pressured him into doing so, we had a real "portrait" done at Ina Sigfried Studios. It was the height of 1968 fancy—all dark wood paneling, heavy drapery backdrops, and lots and lots of lights. I, the budding young actor, thought it was heaven. It took forever to shoot a family portrait with five kids (the youngest wasn't born yet). I have no doubt there were tears involved—there always was some sort of drama with pig tails, Mary Jane's, grey flannel pants, and button down shirts. And I seem to remember a cigarette smoke haze in the studio that wafted under the hot lights Ina Sigfried had set up—it was still the 60s and smoking was encouraged just about everywhere. And I was fascinated by Ina Sigfried, whose very name conjured in my seven-year-old brain a sense of exotic mystery. She even had a German accent, for Pete's sake! Being the goody-goody of the family, I was all ear-to-ear with smiles, wearing my grey flannel shorts, sitting on a stool with my legs crossed at the knees princess-style looking happy as a clam without a hint irony—just enjoying the spotlight. My much more worldly siblings, even my youngest sister, all seem to be in on some sort of inside joke. They seemed to know, even then, the end result would be like a Fellini still. "Merry Christmas from the Andersons!"

In the years after that, there were many, many more cards, but none were as fancy as the year we went to Ina Sigfried's Studio. My parents have all of them collected and framed in their new apartment in Florida, and it really is amazing to see how the family grew and changed. You can almost write the story of our lives just from looking at the images we collected at those moments each year growing up.

Ok, so come see us, and warm up with some good soup!

1967 Anderson Christmas Card taken at Ina Sigfried Studio. Jamestown, NY

SUNDAY JANUARY 15, 2012

Last night I remembered the joy. Being on stage in front of a friendly, enthusiastic, full house, doing a really lovely play, telling a great story, making people laugh, cry, and think—was awesome! For me, who used to feed on this kind of adrenaline, it was a little like taking out an old Armani suit from the closet, one that you loved back in the day, but haven't worn in a while. You slip it on and it fits around you like the arms of an old, long-lost friend. I had a blast. We absolutely peaked at the right time, and the show was flawless—at least from my perspective. Richie said it's the best thing he's ever seen me in, and after 15 years of dragging him to my shows about everything from 18th Century English Poets to Harold Pinter theatre of "pauses", he's in a good position to have an opinion. Of course, it could be just seeing me in that well fitted suit, was, for him, the same feeling. I'm thrilled to be doing it and thankful that my awesome staff allowed their Poppa to step out of the MetroFresh world for just a little while.

THURSDAY JANUARY 27, 2012

I've lost the Battle of the Bed! Perhaps some of you will remember that up until a few months ago, I was summarily being pushed out the bed by our rather zaftig cat, Elmo, who liked to stretch out as big as can be, smack dab in the middle. Well, sadly, Elmo is no longer with us, but he has been replaced by an even bigger animal. About a month ago, Richie decided it was time for Schotzi to get a big girl bed and put the kennel in the garage. She'd been sleeping soundly in her little house for three years without a problem. So, who knows why the system had to change. But it did. Maybe you should ask a Gemini. Richie went out and bought a comfy, fluffy bed for her and, well, she does sleep on it... for about half an hour! You can put her in before lights out and somehow, after she senses we are deep in REM, she sneaks her way up onto the big boy bed. And for some reason, she ALWAYS gets in on MY SIDE. I wake up in the middle of the night and she has managed to sprawl out on the lower two thirds, making no room for my rather long legs. I'm force to curl up like a ball. I get frustrated and try as hard as I can to nudge her off; who knew a 50-lb. sleeping dog would be so hard to move. I push and push, and she doesn't seem to care! Then, as if she's trying to make ME look bad, by morning she's sleeping soundly over in HER bed like nothing ever happened. Richie thinks I'm making the whole thing up and I've lost my mind. Maybe they're both trying to gaslight me and send me packing off to the loony bin so they can have Anderpino Park all to themselves. It's a plot I tell you—it's a damn plot!

Sweet, sweet Schotzi all grown up and looking fine

THURSDAY APRIL 5, 2012

Hope Spring Break is going well for all of you spring breakers. We certainly have seen our share at the garden over the last few days.

Spring break was one of the great joys of life. In the sixties and seventies, my very large family would get in the Ford Limited Wood-paneled station wagon and go all sorts of places—Niagara Falls, Washington, D.C., West Virginia (don't ask), Florida, and even Myrtle Beach. My favorite trip ever was to New York City with the Griffins. I'm quite sure there were about 300 people who packed into the back of the station wagon for the seven hour trip to the Big Apple. That was back in the days when you didn't really have to strap yourself in like you were going to the moon. Kids flew all over that car like it was a gymnasium. We had sleeping bags and pillows in the "way back" and I seem to recall most of the trip I was in the seat well between the front and back seats.

Anyway, we spent four amazing days in New York. We did every tourist thing you could do, from Mama Leone's (I'm not sure that's even there anymore) to Broadway. The very first Broadway show I ever saw was on that spring break. It was "Shenandoah" starring John Cullum, and it was magic. It's what made me want to be an actor. We also saw "Candide" which I loved but didn't understand, and "Grease" which was great, but Dad found it a bit too racy. He walked out because he got embarrassed they were singing about s.e.x and grabbing body parts. Honestly, just thinking about that spring break makes me smile. It's one of those memories I can piece together in actual snapshots in my mind.

So let's talk about Easter Sunday Brunch, people. We're doing it, and it's going to be great. The Easter Bunny will be here, Rockstar will be here, I'm going to try to be here if I can get away from the garden. It's a favorite day and I hope you'll join us.

THURSDAY MAY 17, 2012

So today is my 15th anniversary. Richie and I met at the Human Rights Campaign Dinner 15 years ago today and we quite literally have been together ever since. Through long distance (the first five years we commuted between LA and Atlanta), career changes, moves, renovations, births and deaths—we've had a great life together.

Richie and I are not exactly alike. In some respects we're opposites—if you know both of us you know what I'm talking about. But the thing that makes it work is that every day we get up and look at the world the same way. I think that's what makes a successful partnership. You may open your eyes in the morning and even if your frames are different, when you have a partner with the same basic lenses, it just works. He's my most cheerful cheerleader and my most ardent supporter. He's the most courageous and kind person I've ever known. He's taught me

Richie as Mitchell, and Mitchell as Richie – Opposites attract!

that risk is only a matter of degrees and the joy of reward is always better when you just believe. How lucky am I!

Come see us today. We'll be here working hard so you don't have to.

MONDAY AUGUST 20, 2012

So you know what I learned over the weekend? Are you ready for this? I am NOT, as previously thought, perfect. It's very hard to admit and I'm having a little crisis inside my belly about it, but it's irrefutable because the evidence is in. And you know? It feels kind of good. It's sort of a release. 51 years old and I finally know what imperfection feels like.

Here's what happened. We had a lovely evening planned at the theatre with our friend Betsy. I was all dressed up in some swanky new duds—new shirt, new pants, new shoes—that Richie got me for my birthday. We picked Betsy up at her house in Sherwood Forest at 6pm. By 6:05 I was shirtless, on the side of Robin Hood, or Doncaster, or Maid Marion or one of those Sherwood Forest character streets, changing a tire on Richie's Audi. I was driving and, somehow the very sharp curb jumped out at me and darned if I didn't rip the tire to shreds. Agh. This was bad on so many levels since I am, like my sisters, not a very good passenger when Richie is driving. This is something that, as he said, if he did would have resulted in some consternation on my part. When I'm driving, OMG, it's a nightmare. Yep, Mr. Perfect made a

bad error which nearly derailed the evening. Fortunately, I know my way around a jack and I got to work changing the offending tire right away. It only took 15 minutes and about a gallon of sweat (which since I had taken my shirt off did not soak the new threads.) We returned to Betsy's to wash the black grease off my hands, dry my torso, and redo my hair and were back on the road—this time with Richie behind the wheel since I was sulking. All turned out well, but my lesson was learned and I'll be purchasing a shiny new tire. Happy birthday to me. And the bonus was we had a delightful night at the Addams Family with my friend Douglas Sills who was wonderful as Gomez Addams.

FRIDAY SEPTEMBER 14, 2012

Good Early Morning to you. Normally on a Friday of Concert Day I wouldn't have time to write the daily message. I start about 100mph when my feet hit the ground and I don't stop. But today is special and I wanted to take a moment to make an announcement. I wanted to put the rumors, the speculation, the "talk" to rest since I finally can. It's been killing us, because until yesterday we couldn't officially talk about it. It's been especially killing Richie who is like a kid in the back seat asks every ten miles "Are we there yet?"

Well, I can finally announce that we are there. I have signed a lease agreement to take over the Jersey Mike's space next door!!!! It's been just about the worst kept secret in Midtown and I know many of you have seen me walking around carrying rolled up plans and talking to designers and contractors over the last month. I wasn't exactly hiding it. But I didn't really want to formally announce it until the ink was dry on the Letter of Intent, which I signed yesterday.

So we will begin work on doubling the size of the restaurant in October. The plan right now is to start demoing the space ASAP and begin construction on the other side most likely in the first of October. The whole project will take about eight weeks and I'm hoping to have it done by December 1st. We are both expanding the dining capacity (to 48 seats) and the doubling the size of the kitchen. It's going to be MetroFresh 2.0. Lindsay Denman and Clint Bearden have been designing their hearts out and the new and improved MetroFresh will have a day and night feel. We're adding a little wine bar/cappuccino/dessert bar, a second register, a new cooking area and a huge new walk in refrigerator. This will give us the ability to expand Rockstar Breakfast in the morning, and be more of a destination hang out restaurant at night.

It's all very exciting and I had to take a few deep breaths before actually signing on the dotted line, As you can see most of the time we are just sort of bursting at the seams both in front and back of the house. We really couldn't continue to do what we have been doing without making this move. The opportunity was there. The door was opened and we walked through it. I'll keep you posted on the progress and put up some renderings next week on what the new space will look like, so stay tuned.

I gotta go. Have a great day!

WEDNESDAY OCTOBER 10, 2012

Today is a special day! Not that every day at MetroFresh isn't special, but today is EXTRA special. Seven years ago today we started this amazing journey called MetroFresh. In some ways I can't believe it's already been

Soledad and Mitchell

seven years, and in some ways it seems that MetroFresh has always just been.

Here's how it worked that day. I had spent the few weeks prior to opening putting the finishing touches on the buildout. Since money was scarce I served as GC, handyman, touch up painter, and accountant. I also was preparing the new restaurant's menu and feel. I met with my staff, we trained, talked about what we wanted MetroFresh to be, and then on October 10, 2005 we opened the doors for our first day. And we haven't stopped since. We were blessed immediately with the best family of customers we could ask for. Our friends in Midtown, Ansley, VA/Hi and beyond came and supported us from the first day and embraced us with more love than we could have imagined. Our goal was not only to make awesome food, but also be like you were walking into my kitchen. My grandmother always said, "No matter where I serve my guests, it seems they like my kitchen best." That's what I wanted MetroFresh to feel like and I think that's what we have always been.

That first day was exciting and exhausting. I worked from about 4am to 11pm. At that moment I didn't have a dishwasher at night. When I got home Richie, who had been my biggest champion, my greatest PR agent, and lived through the highs and lows of starting a new business with me, said, "You'll NEVER be there until 11pm again scrubbing pots." So the next morning I went over to Mellow Mushroom's kitchen and asked if ANYONE knew ANYONE who needed a job immediately. That afternoon Soledad walked through the door and she literally has never left. She, in many ways, is the heart of MetroFresh.

I am blessed with the greatest team in all of Atlanta. Rockstar came in a couple years after we opened and his dedication, talent, good nature, and friendship has made it possible for me to look to other projects like MetroFresh in the Garden and now our newest adventure—our expansion. Thanks to him, Tio Miguel, Diane (who except for a year absence has been here for the whole time as well), and the rest of my incredible staff for seven amazing years and here's to a lucky seven more! Come see us and celebrate.

WEDNESDAY DECEMBER 26, 2012

Well, Christmas is over for another year. We had a great day made even better because I didn't have to work. I have an awesome team at the Garden who handled the few who came to see the lights yesterday and aside from dropping off a Santa present for each of them, I didn't step foot in a MetroFresh location for the whole day. I made a traditional dinner with Roast Beef and Yorkshire pudding, fingerling potatoes and fresh green beans. Richie fluffed the table into a stupor and we had a few friends for dinner. Lots of laughs, a few tears of gratitude, some singing and even Jake Goldwasser on his sax! I'm not all that chipper today, but it was totally worth it.

MetroFresh before the renovation

MetroFresh 2.0 after the renovation

So you'll notice we're NOT closed as planned today—nor will we be until further notice. Mr. McScrooge in the "Site Development" division at the city is now holding up our permit because of grease traps. It's all news to me, since I had my current trap inspected, showed the nice man from Watershed management what we were going to do, and all he said was, "You're fine." Apparently we're not fine, and if we can't or don't want to install a huge 1500 gallon grease trap somewhere in the parking lot, we have to have a grease "interceptor" at each sink. I asked him if this was a new code and he said no. So when I asked him how I was able to open seven years ago with only one grease trap, he said "I don't know."

So it's back to the engineers to draw up yet another set of plans that include grease interceptors at each prep sink, the mop sink, even the little sink under the new bar that is only going to wash glassware! And, there is a chance that he will nix the whole thing if he decides my equipment is too much and will produce too much grease and then we'll be back in the parking lot. I'm not going there yet, but, honestly, I don't know how much more of this I can take. So new plan is...

We'll be open this week through Monday at 4pm (New Year's Eve), closed on New Year's Day, and then reopen on the second of January. My contractors are going to do what they can to minimize the impact on our business when (and if) we ever get our permits. They'll complete most of the work next door and then we'll close most

likely toward the middle/end of January for only a few days. He's convinced he can do it fast.

So the saga, sadly, continues. I am now on the other side of it and just looking at the future with a shiny new MetroFresh—hopefully by February.

Come see us today and tonight. We'll be here to give you some great LIGHT food, and keep you healthy throughout the Christmas week.

WEDNESDAY JANUARY 16, 2013

Good news! We are getting our building permit TODAY! Apparently we have kissed the right rings and genuflected the correct amount of times. Yesterday afternoon, I received an email from the Associate Director of Buildings informing me they were going to issue the permit today. Of course I am relieved, of course I am happy that our long nightmare has come to a close and we can begin the renovation, but it came with such heartache it's hard not to carry a little bit of resentment into the joy.

Yesterday, after doing my civic duty and showing up for jury duty, I went into City Hall to talk to Mr. Thomas, who had been sitting on our grease trap plans for more than two weeks. He came out of his office with the huge stack of plans wrapped in comments saying, "The information required was not provided." Naturally I was dumbfounded. That was simply impossible. He told me there were only architectural plans in the roll and no plumbing plans. "That's not right," I told him, "Why would we resubmit our plans without giving you what you asked for?" So I unrolled the stack and sure enough, the four sets of plumbing plans he needed were on the bottom. Apparently he just couldn't be bothered to go through the whole stack. I'm guessing the action of flipping through ALL the plans would have put him at too high of a risk for a paper cut and he just didn't look! You think I'm making this up, I know, but sadly, I am not. I showed him the plans he needed and he said he would look at them yesterday afternoon and send them downstairs. And I guess he was appropriately embarrassed enough to actually follow through since by 5pm there was the email from the Associate Director. So there, it's finally done and we will begin work as early as this afternoon on the project, just three months after we first submitted the plans to the city.

I know I shouldn't look a gift horse in the mouth. And I am grateful we are finally able to start, but it goes without saying this "victory" was ugly. It just simply should not be that difficult to get a building permit in the City of Atlanta for a 1250 square foot expansion of an existing business. After all, I am not building a condo! Anyway, let's move on and look forward. I will have a better idea today after we meet with the contractor and subs what our final schedule will be. They will work practically around the clock to get this done quickly. Hopefully the inspection process happens with less stress and delay than the approval process. So let's all get excited as MetroFresh 2.0 finally becomes a reality.

MONDAY JUNE 10, 2013

Where to start? On Friday I headed north to Williamstown, MA for my 30th college reunion (a number I still find slightly stunning)!

I was prepared for a great weekend. I was not prepared for an EPIC weekend. I had a blast. From the moment I walked on campus until the moment I left, I jibber-jabbered with about 200 of my amazing classmates. The class of 1983 from Williams College truly was exceptional—and I'm sure every class would say that. But here are people, now solidly in their middle age at 52ish, doing amazing things, living life with all of its ups and downs, coming back to reunion both

With my best college friend Dan Flaherty before graduation 1983

embolden by the power of age and humbled by the passing of time. My friend Alice Albright (daughter of former Secretary of State Madeline) just returned from a two week trip to Africa working, as she says, in the Education Sector, promoting education reform in the developing world. This was after a four year stint in the Obama Administration working on poverty issues. Not to be out done, Rob and Dina Bowman had just returned from four years in Ethiopia and Kenya where Rob was a lawyer for the State Department and Dina is a political appointee for USAID. They took all three of their children for the adventure of a lifetime. We have professors, many doctors, researchers in physics, writers and poets. But the thing is, not only are these people interesting and accomplished, they are interested in everyone else's accomplishments. And yet, even with all these amazing stories, there truly was a feeling that big or small, life is the journey and no matter where you find yourself at our age, just getting here is the story. We mourned the loss of several classmates over the last five years and this main story of life lived came ever more into stark relief. Everyone pretty much looked the same with a few more wrinkles and lots more gray hair. One guy, John McClellan, even rode his bike from BOSTON—11 hours in the pouring rain. Ok, I found that a little irritating.

The best was Saturday night when The Doctors, a cover band of classmates, who played all the parties in the early 80s, got back together for a one night only concert. We all danced like we were freshman. And if that wasn't enough, we made our way to the one bar in town and continued to dance until 2:30am! Next to me were my best friends. Daniel, his wife Beth, Roger and Liz, John, Austin, Heidi and so many more just having fun. We missed our dear Katy Miller (see above), who passed away a couple years ago and was our heart and soul, but I know she was up there looking down with that incredible perma-grin and laughing with us. Ok, so I didn't feel all that pretty yesterday morning. But to have that moment, at that moment in my life, with those incredible people, just having fun was worth every Advil in the bottle!

I feel incredibly fortunate to have gone to Williams. My parents made it possible and there is not a day that goes by I don't recognize their sacrifice and dedication to my education that made it possible. We left yesterday with promises of returning in five years for the 35th. I'm guessing there won't be another 2:30am dance marathon, but I'll go again if only to be reminded that these people are exceptional, kind, generous, and a whole lot of fun.

SATURDAY JULY 20, 2013

In a world full of heroes, my staff has to rank toward the top. We put out some FOOD! Yesterday at the sold out Boz Scaggs concert in the Garden, we plated and sold over

1600 individual plates. That's monumental. But what's more, is that we were efficient, organized, and ready to go about an hour before the doors opened! No kidding. We had over 250 pre-orders, which is amazing and takes an army to put into bags and organized so that when the throngs of excited Boz Scaggers (that doesn't sound pretty) arrive all at once, it's not total chaos getting their orders. On top of that we have food to sell on table tops, and sold it we did! Richie was "the guy" as we like to call him, who greets the guests at the door and asks them "Are you picking up a pre-order or are you shopping?" They come in like a tsunami between 7:05 and 7:30 so it's no easy task. He directs them to the proper place and makes them laugh as they enter what looks to be yet another over-crowded cluster f***, which if you know what you're doing is not at all that, but a well organized machine. And he did it great! He said he had a blast and we might, if I buy him just enough red wine, come back for another appearance or two!

Then, the pre-order happens. With 250 people all arriving at the same time—some with their order numbers, some without, it's kind of like running a marathon in circles a few hundred times! We have four pickers and Jamie and I checking people in. We do it the best we can, and if the line gets just a little longer than the pre orderers would like, we remind them that they are standing in a lovely 69 degree Day Hall and the longer they stay, the more comfortable

they'll be as they make their way to the great lawn to settle in hot summer's eve.

At any rate, Poppa is about to drop this morning. I'm completely satisfied and I did want to give a shout out to all my staff who help make this all work. It's really something to see. Sarah especially. She has taken over the management of the whole affair and on her end, there is absolutely nothing missing or out of place. Everyone knows their role and everyone has a smile on their face. I had several people tell me how great they were—how helpful and friendly and it is mostly because Sarah is that way and sets the tone.

THURSDAY AUGUST 15, 2013

I had a thought this morning. I heard that the Lohan (as in Lindsey) is getting out of her sixth stay in rehab and going straight to Oprah's couch. I had one of those super long days yesterday and early mornings this morning, and I'm kinda wasted. And I thought, maybe I should go to rehab. Now, don't get all mad at me, I know rehab is serious and I'm not...but doesn't it sound relaxing? Maybe like 8-14 weeks in some cushy Malibu all-star rehab. I mean, what would I have to do? Isn't it a lot of sitting around talking and, as my father used to say, contemplating life? I assume there is a bed—with sheets. Maybe the bathroom is down the hall, but someone is going to cook your meals, and it really seems like it could be relaxing and philosophically rewarding. I don't have an addiction problem, but I could make one up... like the friend of mine who went to rehab at a Canyon Ranch-like place in Santa Fe and discovered she was addicted to love (That's no lie! That really happened). I'm picturing long walks, pithy books, and forced lights out by 8:30pm. Ah...that would be the life!

Well, maybe if I just cut out a little early today and fall asleep on the couch...that'll be just as good and then I'll be all refreshed and ready for the busy weekend!

Anyway—come see us today. It's a little like fall out there so doesn't soup sound good?

TUESDAY AUGUST 20, 2013

So Richie and I are getting on a plane tomorrow for a very mini vacation to points north. We're spending a night in a fancy hotel in Toronto, where we'll find some sort of awesome restaurant and try to stay up to find some kind of bar/nightclub to celebrate. And then we go to camp! I've talked about it before, but let me fill you in.

I went to and worked at a camp in Algonquin Park, some three hours north of Toronto for all of my child-hood, teen years, and into college. Pathfinder is well rooted in Anderson family tradition. Literally every male member of my family, my dad and his five brothers, my cousins, nephews and brothers went there. It is the place that defined me as a person and I am incredibly lucky to be part of that amazing tradition. We are going

The third generation of Pathfinder campers – Nephews, Andreas, Colin and Ben

A flock of Andersons on Pathfinder Island, August 2013

back to celebrate Pathfinder's 100 years. I'm excited to have Richie see the island, hear the loons on the lake at night, and maybe even catch the northern lights on a late night paddle. To dive in the cool clear waters of Source Lake is to know a little bit of heaven. Pathfinder not only connected me to amazing people and experience in the wild, but rooted me in the tradition of being an Anderson. At the end of the camping season, awards are given to various campers who have excelled in their age groups. There are two biggies—the Pathfinder Award and the Tripping Award. The winner is put on a plaque on the wall. My father won both big awards in 1944 and 1945 and his name is up there along with my Uncle Tim, my cousins Trip and Josh, my nephews Ben and Sam, and me! The Pathfinder legacy is alive and well in our family, and I can't think of a better way to spend my 52nd birthday than visiting Pathfinder Island, where standing under the tall pines makes you feel at once tiny in the scheme of nature and a giant in the legacy of something important. We'll drink lots of beer, sing lots of camp songs (some of which Richie knows because I sing them all the time), and laugh a lot with old friends.

MONDAY AUGUST 26, 2013

I could write for hours this morning about my weekend at Camp Pathfinder in Algonquin Park, Ontario. It would be one of those long blog posts that you'd want to read, but know you should go back to your work (and know that I should be working too to catch up from a few days away). So I'll try to sum it all up in just a paragraph (or maybe two).

Arriving at Source Lake on Thursday night was a little like how Dorothy must have felt when she arrived in OZ. When you arrive, you park at the "Car Dock" and have to be shuttled via boat to your destination.

On the swim dock ready to jump!

Thursday night we stayed at my friend Sue Werner's cottage, which is across from Pathfinder Island. You round the first point and have the most amazing view of the whole lake. The late afternoon sun was sparkling on the rippled waves, the white puffy clouds were marching slowly across the sky, and it truly was the end of the rainbow. Richie sat there in silent amazement. We had an awesome night at Sue's with my sister and her family and then Saturday morning went over to camp. Stepping on the island for the first time in many years was like stepping into the back door of your favorite house. I was home. And the oddest thing, Richie felt like he was home as well. To be sure, it's super rustic. Basically, the physical look of the camp hasn't changed since my father was there in the 1930s and 40s. The trees are taller, but everything else was just like it was when my dad walked the same hallowed trails. And then the "campers" started arriving. And honestly, whether I had ever met them or not, they were all my friends. And lots of my friends were there. And, yes, then the beer drinking, the stories, and the laughter began. It didn't stop until we left yesterday at noon.

So quickly now, because I know you have to get back to work. The spirit and energy of the camp has not changed; if anything, it has grown stronger in the 100 years of its existence. The big camp "meeting" had amazing speeches about the past, present, and future of the camp. After the second speaker, who happens to be a PhD Math professor in Chattanooga, and was my greatest influence as a child and young adult, Richie turned to me, tears rolling down from beneath his sunglasses and said, "Now I understand why you are such a good guy!" And my weekend was made.

Camp Pathfinder is a rare and amazing place. And my mother and father, through no small sacrifice, found a way to send my two brothers and me there summer after summer because his parents had done the same. Brooks, my younger and more eloquent brother, was given a couple minutes on stage to read an email from dad which expressed his sadness that he was unable to come to the reunion (more tears anyone?). But in a few simple words, dad found the wisdom to sum up what it all means. Whether you're eight or eighty, Pathfinder remains one of the greatest forces in your life. And yes, it really did mold us into who we are right now.

TUESDAY SEPTEMBER 3, 2013

So I have some news for y'all. We have made a very important decision that I want to share. My contract with the garden is up at the end of the year and after a couple months of discussion with Richie, Rockstar and Sarah, we have decided that we won't seek to renew. Believe me I didn't come to this conclusion easily or without a lot of thought. I have found that running two restaurants, even when they are spitting distance from one another, is incredibly time consuming, to say the least. I have worked six or seven days a week for the last couple of years without very much down time. At the end of the day I just decided I want to enjoy my life a little bit more and maybe not work quite as hard. The last three years have been great and we have learned so much, accomplished so much, and I don't regret the time at all. But now, perhaps, it's time for Poppa to get a life outside of work. We have created such a great space in the midtown shop, I want to enjoy it, be here more, see you all daily and even explore other exciting options. Maybe there is a cookbook in the future. Maybe we can have more cooking classes. Maybe we'll have more music and wine nights. And maybe, I'll restring my tennis racket and play once a week. It's just time to pull back and enjoy what we've created. I certainly thank ABG for the opportunity they gave MetroFresh three years ago and I know they'll find a great vendor to take our place. But I'm so looking forward to 2014 and all the new possibilities it will bring!

WEDNESDAY OCTOBER 9, 2013

I really want to write something that contains a little bit of wisdom, a dose of pathos, a splash of humor, and maybe just a teaspoon of irony. But the words aren't coming out in just that way. I'm, for once in my life, at a loss for words.

The aging process, while part of life, is really hard to watch. It's even harder, I'm certain, to experience. Last week was tough. I spent many hours in the hospital next to my mother, who, as you know, has had one thing after another this summer/fall. I won't go into details, but the last one was awful. She's confused and hurting and no amount of reassurance, no amount of outpoured love in her direction, can help her get through this. Yes, she has a certain level of dementia, but there is that innate feeling in her whole being that something is wrong! She's only peaceful when she's sleeping. The rest of the time she wrestles with equal amounts of pain and confusion. It's incredibly frustrating and sad. Through it all, I'm trying to remind myself that it's her that is going through this, not me. I also realize we all, in one way or another, will go through this at some point. But for those of us watching from the sidelines (my father, my siblings, her

My beautiful mother on her wedding day. June 5, 1954

caregivers) our hearts are breaking. I guess the hope is, as she heals from this surgery, she will be able to live relatively pain free, but beyond that, who knows? The good news is that her care is excellent and for now at least, she's home, where she can experience at least some level of comfort.

SATURDAY OCTOBER 12, 2013

Ah, Gay Pride Weekend. So here's the thing about Gay Pride when you're in your fifties, having been "out" for 30 something years, lived through the devastating and scary 80s and early 90s when all your friends were sick and dying, been on the stump demanding fairness, acceptance, tolerance, respect (or at least a life free of the fear of violence, discrimination, bigotry), stepped off the stump, helped the survivors survive another day and be healthy, lived long enough to see POTUS actually support marriage equality and allow gays and lesbians to serve openly in the military, see the Supremes vote to end a certain amount of federal unfairness in our marriages, and a dozen or so states issue actual marriage licenses to same sex couples: you experience "Gay Pride" on a much different level. You've been there, done that. You've marched, cheered, cried, and laughed—and yes, you've partied your ASS off at the festival. But now, Pride to me is just another weekend of fun in a big city that welcomes everyone. It is a living, modern example of inclusion, and I bet

if you go to the festival or parade tomorrow you'll see all sorts of people, Gay, straight, young, old, highly political, apathetic, big partiers, families, the raver kids, and the laid back adults. And here we are in 2013, and we've really changed. This is not to say that intransigent pockets of horrible bigotry and hatred are not out there. It's just to say that the weekend is really about a celebration of diversity that's not only ok, it's great. It's the American character (albeit on display to the max in some cases.) It's the Dykes on Bikes and Leather Daddies as well as the Gay Moms and Dads with their kids, and PFlag, and Out, Gay and Married Veterans (how amazing is that?). And yes, there will be that one annoying group at the entrance of Piedmont Park saying we all are going to hell, but we'll just walk on by and shower them with the love we feel—isn't that what Jesus Christ said to do? Because that's what it's about.

Nowadays, I'm well passed the speechifying. I feel that Richie and I live our lives in what I call the "Quiet Activism of Every Day Life." It's an open and lovely life, free of drama (they're not going to call US for a reality TV program). But it's a life we can actually be proud of, because not only is there nothing to hide, there is everything to celebrate. We've been together now for 16 years. We have a real life together, we support each other in our dreams, our joy and our sadness, and our businesses; we take care of the dog and the cat, we enjoy our neighbors and our customers and they enjoy us. Not because we're that nice novel 'gay couple' up the street, but because we are a living, breathing, and yes, excitingly boring couple that just lives their lives in the open. That is the Activism of Every Day Life. That is how I now choose to live—is there really any other way? And ultimately that is how we, as a movement, have made it so far. That's why today is SO much different than 1983 when I first came out. And that's why I'm proud!

But I'll be at the festival tonight having fun—watching the people and drinking a tall can of Miller Lite (where exactly do they get cans that tall?) And I'll be enjoying the diversity all the way. Maybe we can get Fred Phelps here to kick back with a beer and listen to some good music. Then maybe he won't be SO angry and see us as the enemy.

MONDAY OCTOBER 14, 2013

My mom was a scofflaw!

One Columbus Day back in the early 70s (I know, it seems like a long time ago), my mom and her best lady friends, Aunt Carol, Aunt Mary, and Aunt Ginny (not real relations but like second, third, and fourth mothers to us) took all their kids to Long Point State Park on Chautauqua Lake. It was a lovely Indian summer day, the leaves were changing, the air was crisp, and there was the smell of charred hot dogs in the air.

And there wasn't anyone else there.

So for some reason, Sandy, Carol, Mary, and Ginny decided that it would be ok to let the older kids—and by older I mean the 14 and 15 year olds—get behind the wheel of the various Ford Limited wood paneled station wagons and tool around the parking lot. I was only about 9 or 10, so this did not include me. But it was quite the event for my sisters and the other older kids. It was fairly safe, and I'm sure they didn't go much over 20 mph.

And all was good, until...

Oops, darned if the park ranger didn't come down the drive to check on things. Caught! Apparently, it didn't matter that there was no one else in the park and the parking lot was empty. The ranger was not at all impressed with the driving skill of the underage motorists. Nor was he impressed with the huge, if momentary, lack of judgment displayed by my mom and her cohorts. What were they thinking?

I don't think anything serious happened—no one was hauled off to jail, but I seem to remember a call to

The Four Instigators - Mary, Jinny, Sandy, Carol

my dad and my Uncle Sherry, who happened to be the family lawyer. I believe tickets were given and paid and the incident went into the family history as "just one of those silly things!" Anyway, that's what I was thinking about this morning on Columbus Day.

SUNDAY OCTOBER 20, 2013

So I'm not going to say that I'm proud of my little restaurant for hosting the Grady High School Chorus fund raiser last night because I know that pride is a deadly sin punishable by an eternity of burning. And, of course, it's Sunday, so that would be even worse. But I have to say, last night I was, as my Jewish friends would say, "kvelling" more than just a little. The cafe was alive with the sound of music and the spirit of community. My parents taught us that being an integral part of the community is what life is all about. They taught us that it's not enough to just give back, but that immersion in your cultural surroundings is essential for success. And I'm not talking about financial success, that's boring and mundane. I'm talking about spiritual success. So last night, with all these young singers from Grady Chorus entertaining us on the patio to raise money for their spring trip to New York City, was all about the spiritual enhancement of my life and the life of MetroFresh. All I could think was, I wish Mom and Dad could have been there to both enjoy the music and see how MetroFresh has been able to find life and

love within the community in which we live. I loved it, and having participated in the chorus being able to raise over $2500 in one night, well, OK, I know mom and dad would be proud. And they're allowed to be proud 'cause parents just are. And heck, I'm allowed to kvell just a little.

SATURDAY NOVEMBER 16, 2013

It was like a 1940s slapstick comedy yesterday when I broke myself!

I decided to do a little gardening in front of the restaurant—time to pull up the potato vines and replant the window boxes. That all went fairly well, but I had also decided to wear adult clothes, i.e., brand new items from the GAP Outlet store in Vero Beach. So there I was, working away in the dirt, making a mess. All was going fairly well, when I further decided to finally pull out that dead tree in the big planter inside the patio. That thing has been irritating me for months and months. So I worked it around, got it good and loose and then... pulled, pulled, and pulled. Finally it came loose...

...On top of me, on my back, on the patio floor.

Chairs and tables went flying, I was covered with dirt, and my pride was wounded. PJ and Sarah, who must have caught the calamity out the corners of their eyes, came a-running. I got up, dusted myself off, and then for the rest of the day, my 52-year-old body was completely out of whack! It's not too bad today, but those kinds of things, as you get older, manage to break you. Even for a day.

MONDAY DECEMBER 16, 2013

I read this interesting opinion piece in the New York Times yesterday about happiness, about how we are always in its pursuit and how many of us actually get there. Most people tie their happiness to their work, which I thought was interesting and pretty much true. I remember back in my acting days, no matter how much I tried not to, I always seemed to tie my happiness to whether I was working or not. When someone asked, "How are you?", I hated answering it when work was

Christmas with just four – 1964

scarce. When I was booking jobs... yay. When I wasn't, I generally couldn't come up with a decent answer. Part of the happiness equation is rooted in security and a good source of income is primary. So a career in show business that is by its nature feast or famine is a really difficult path to happiness. However, as the article says, if you root your pursuit of happiness in faith, family, community, AND meaningful work, then you have more direct path to happiness.

I read this article after spending some of my day off here at MetroFresh. Rockstar, Brad, and the rest of the staff were all doing great and I didn't have to rush off to the other restaurant with supplies or put out any fires; I was able to just enjoy MetroFresh. I had lovely conversations with several people who I see all the time, but rarely have five extra minutes to chat with. I had a great brunch with Richie and it made me happy! There it was—maybe not faith, but community, family, and meaningful work (actually there's a little faith in there, too) and happiness was in my grasp.

Come see us and be happy!

TUESDAY DECEMBER 24, 2013

And it came to pass in a stable in the town of Bethlehem... Well, you know the rest. Merry Christmas MetroFreshuals young and old, far and near.

My parents knew how to throw DOWN on Christmas. And I'm not talking about Christmas dinner, where the adults, and most of the older kids, managed to consume cases upon cases of burgundy champagne. I'm talking about Christmas morning. It was for me the most exciting day of the year. I wasn't a particularly spoiled child and I wasn't a gimme gimme gimme kind of kid, but I remember the anticipation of Christmas morning built like a snowball rolling down a hill in the days before. I remember having butterflies in my stomach. It was almost too much for a little boy to handle.

In our house, Santa didn't wrap gifts. This was, no doubt, due to the fact that with six kids and all the gifts between us, it would have taken poor old St. Nick weeks of work and mountains of paper to do it. Somehow, Mom and Dad (I mean Santa) managed to accumulate stacks of presents for each one of us without a hint of them ever doing it. We'd wake up Christmas morning and run around to one another's' rooms seeing who was awake. Then we'd sit at the top of the stairs, waiting for Mom and Dad to get out of bed. And when Nana and Grampe were with us, for Nana to put on her make up or ponds cold cream or whatever it was that TOOK HER SO DARN LOOOOONG! So we'd sit and wait. Then dad would go down, light the tree, and say, "Bye Santa, thanks for coming, see you next year!" (He said this every year, no matter what.) Then, he'd get the Super 8 movie camera out, light that enormously bright flood light, and record us coming downstairs, rounding the corner to the living room and searching for our bounty, which was stacked individually on all the furniture in the living room. There are home movies of us, year after year, with enormous smiles as we found our very own pile. We'd spend some time on our own treasures then take a look at everyone else's. This part of the ritual was almost as fun. I remember distinctly actually falling down when I saw my sister Kris' new Head Jr. 90's skis. I thought that was the greatest present in the world.

So the day would proceed; we'd have a great breakfast and then return to the chaos to open presents from each other and from Nana and Grampe. When I think back, I am amazed and grateful at how special the day was. There was always a feeling of abundance, even in years when I know it was a stretch for them to do it. And the last thing was always one more present for the six of us from Mom and Dad, since Santa had provided the rest of the gifts. One year it was a bumper pool table just like they had at the Y. Another year, a new color TV.

Christmas is different now. Richie and I have our own traditions. We enjoy the peaceful quiet of Christmas morning, just the two of us with Schotzi and Pino, drinking coffee, opening presents, and making breakfast. Then I get to work on Christmas dinner and Richie puts on his red velvet coat, a Santa cap, and takes off in the car to give $1 bills to people on the street. It's lovely and sweet and I wouldn't trade it for the world. We always have a few friends over for dinner, which usually means drinking copious amounts of good wine (see above) and enjoying lots of laughs in the annual Chinese Christmas gift exchange where we steel each other's gag gifts—the best/worst ones are always passed around the most. It'll be a great day. And you know? I still get those butterflies as Christmas approaches. Yes, because there's always a lot to do, but mostly because I really do love the day. And for me, it's really about repeating rituals that ground us in family, love and tradition. They remind us of our past and ground us in the present.

Merry Christmas, once again. I hope y'all have a great and peaceful holiday. We'll be closed in the midtown store at 4pm today, tomorrow and Thursday but the rest of the week and weekend will be normal hours. Come see us today and stock up on soup!

FRIDAY DECEMBER 27, 2013

So I have some news. On Christmas morning, after all the gifts were open—I got a new bike and some athletic wear to prepare myself for my new and improved 2014 life when I'm not working every second of every day—I had one more gift for Richie. After 17 years together, and after a year in which the Supremes (the court not the 1960's girl group headed by Miss Diana Ross) decided that marriage, at least on a federal level, ought to be treated the same across the board, I decided to ask Richie if he would honor me with a commitment of marriage. Yep! I got down on one knee, pulled a ring box out of my Christmas pajamas, and put it on his finger! And he said yes!

Now, this decision has been long in coming. Years ago, back in the mid 90s, I was an activist for marriage equality in California. It was the beginning wave of anti-marriage initiatives that swept the nation. I tried to convince people that committed, long term, loving relationships should be both supported by the community

Richie and me on Vancouver Island, BC November 2011

and honored by governments. And that we ought to be afforded the same rights and responsibilities as our brothers and sisters who have the license. Then I moved to Georgia and settled down into a new life. For many years, both Richie and I had the "If it ain't broke don't fix it" mentality. And frankly, since the state of Georgia was so far behind the other 18 states that now recognize marriages, we just didn't think it was possible or worth it to get married. But last year, those barriers changed—especially on a federal level. So not only is the golden ring attainable, I now believe it's important politically and practically to reach out and grab the wedding ring, to tie the knot—even if it happens to be with a license from New York or California or Vermont. Someday our state will catch up, but until then, having that paper that recognizes that Richie and I have a real marriage, as real as anyone's, is important. Now instead of "If it ain't broke, don't fix it," we'll be making stronger what we already have!

We're super excited and as soon as Richie posted it on his Facebook, he received over 500 responses from friends across the country. We'll most likely go up to New York and get a license, have a small gathering for family and friends in the north, and then in the fall, have a ceremony and celebrate in our own back yard! Wow! That's some 2014.

SATURDAY JANUARY 4, 2014

Today is our last day in the Garden! It was a difficult decision to leave, but having made the decision in the middle of the summer, I'm happy the day is here. We gave it our all over the last three years. We learned a lot, met some great people, had our share of stresses—ups and

MetroFresh in the Garden

downs, but for now, I'm thrilled that after three years, I'll be contracting a bit and concentrating on our amazing midtown store. After the renovation last February (it's almost been a year) it was always hard for me to leave here and go there. I love this space and I can't wait to fully realize what we have created. So it's a satisfying day. Rockstar and I worked out the new kitchen schedule and it looks like I'll be in this kitchen three mornings and one evening every week. I'm excited to get back to what I love—the creating part.

THURSDAY JANUARY 23, 2014

So the frigid weather makes me think of my childhood... Growing up in western New York was a challenge for most people during the cold winter months. But in my family, it was awesome! We skiied, built snow forts, and I even had a very lucrative shoveling "route" with the old ladies in the neighborhood. But when it got REALLY cold, in the single digits, that's when my mom would get out the hose and make the most incredible backyard ice rink in the city. I can't tell you it was a regulation hockey rink or anything. No doubt it exists larger in my mind than in reality, but every evening, in the cold still of the arctic air, my mom would bundle up, go outside and lightly spray the cleared space for our rink. There was an art to it and my mom had the artist's touch. It took good four or five nights of frigid temps, but once the base of fine ice was down, it was heaven! We'd be out

there every day after school horsing around on skates, playing broom hockey, and pretending to compete in figure skating championships (I know, kind of a cliché for me). My mom would be in the den handing hot chocolate out the window like it was a concession stand. I'm not kidding you; our backyard was a magnet for pretty much the whole city. Some Saturday afternoons it was like the rink at Piedmont Park, and we didn't know half the people that showed up.

So when I see the thermometer dropping in the dead of winter, I have to smile just a little bit. Mom and Dad made all seasons fun. I guess they had to. Having six children cooped up in the house for months on end, no doubt, would have driven them completely insane. A few nights of freezing her buns off making a skating rink in mid January was probably what kept my mom from going loco.

Skating rink at 4 Ridgley Terrace, Jamestown, NY

THURSDAY APRIL 17, 2014

You know I love my job, right? I'm really proud of the little world we created here. We work hard, we feed lots of people, and (most of the time) we have lots of fun doing it. (More so now since I have more time to enjoy)

But once in a while, someone says something about MetroFresh that makes it even more special—even more meaningful. We have a lovely regular customer, who has been coming to us since we opened so many years ago. The other night, she asked for some strained chicken soup. She had been put on a liquid diet for a few days for a medical reason. Of course, it wasn't a problem to give her some chicken stock from whatever chicken soup we had that day (fortunately it wasn't something like chicken tortilla). I was happy to help. This same woman came in the very next day and asked for some more chicken broth. I really didn't want to pry, but I told her I hoped she was feeling better. She said, "Oh my, yes. As a matter of fact, I have been going through cancer treatment for the last year, and you have been nourishing me the whole time. You've made me feel as well as I can be!"

I've been thinking about this for the whole week and it's just made me smile inside. What a blessing to have a career and a "calling" that really does nourish people in all states of life—when they're well and when they're sick. I think about that too, when our cute elderly ladies come in once a week for their cup soup or when young parents bring their children, serving them the same "adult" goodness they eat. Having been open now for almost 9 years, we've really seen the circle of life right here in the Midtown Promenade. We've had lots of expectant mothers and nervous first time fathers, we've had plenty of people who have been nourished back to health through good, wholesome food, and sadly, but inevitably, we've seen the end of life as well. And that's just perfect.

I'm not sure why today is the day I'm waxing nostalgic and getting all gushy, but, as always, it's just something I was thinking about. I hope you'll come enjoy part of your day with us and let us nourish you.

TUESDAY APRIL 22, 2014

The first "Professional" show I ever did, the first one for which I was paid—not much, but paid nevertheless, was in New York City! I'm not kidding. It was the summer I graduated from college—1983, before I was to begin my Juilliard studies in acting (sounds so hoity toity don't it!) I was a young, energetic wisp of thing, with a pretty good tenor voice and this dream to perform on the NY stage. This show, a cabaret evening of 60's music entitled "And the Beat Goes On" (naturally) played in a club on W 46th street—New York's famed Restaurant Row! I basically arrived in NY, school in my future and a paid gig in my present and I was happy as a little clam. I sang a rousing version of The Monkey's "I'm a Believer", was part of the Mama's and the Poppa's medley singing "Monday, Monday" and others, and did a lovely, simple rendition of "Scarborough Fair", sitting center stage on a stool. Really, it was one of the best times of my life. That show brought the house down every night. We had a blast, the audience sang along, and had I not already enrolled at Juilliard, where outside work was forbidden, I would have stayed in that show for a year.

Anyway, my mind went there last night at THE LION SINGS TONIGHT, the cabaret benefit Richie and I attended at the Woodruff Arts Center. These kids, most of them in their 20s, a few a little older, and 4 adorable pre-teens, just shared this amazing show with all the joy, talent, energy and love they could muster. They work super hard doing 8 shows of the THE LION KING on tour every week. But I know, and I could see it in their performances last night, that these special evenings away from their "Day Job" singing and entertaining for an amazing cause, just reenergizes them and makes them happy. The show was awesome and we had a blast.

I'm not particularly sad about getting older. In so many ways the 52 year old version of me is SO much better than the 22 year old one. But last night at the show and later on in the silent darkness of 3am when Schotzi was hogging the bed and I couldn't move or sleep, I started thinking about that wonderful energy one has at the beginning of adulthood. I'm sure at the time there was significant angst, and I know from working with that age group on a daily basis, the present is SO DAMN IMPORTANT that nothing else seems to matter. The passion of the moment completely overwhelms the calmness that comes with perspective (read age.) But

boy, do I miss that energy—that optimism, that sense that everything is out there in front of you.

I love my life now, no question about it. I don't write this with any sense of melancholy or sadness. But once in a while, it's great to be reminded of those days, of the possibility that exists when every experience is new, and that, at one time, life was not necessarily rational, but deliciously unbalanced and carefree.

That's a long one today. See what happens when I have an extra five minutes on my hands? I hope you'll come see us today. We have a great menu, and we'll try our best to make you smile. Have a great day!

THURSDAY MAY 15, 2014

I started writing a couple of weeks ago! I'm not that far along, but my cookbook is underway. I figure if I talk about it, make plans for a release date, and then just work diligently, when time permits, one step after another, I'll get it done. I had a couple hours in the office yesterday, where it's quiet, and I just wrote. Who knows if what I wrote so far will even make it in the book, but I was musing about my culinary influences. I was writing about my two grandmothers.

First, my dad's mother, who was sort of the classic Americana definition of grandma. White hair, a little stout, and just about the most loving person in the world! I won't give too much away, but I remember her making Sunday dinner of a standing rib roast, oven

With grandma at Heidi's wedding

With Nana at my college graduation

roasted potatoes, steamed fresh green beans, Yorkshire pudding and baked Alaska and then, as though it was nothing, calling it "Catch as catch can!" In truth I never exactly knew what that phrase meant. She was just an easy, wonderful Betty Crocker type cook.

And then my mom's mother, Nana, who was more Kathryn Hepburn—tall, erect, slender, regal, and kind of fancy. She was much more of a gourmand, the Julia Child kind of cook, who didn't make spaghetti sauce, she made Bolognaise! She didn't throw a roast in the oven she made Boef Bourguigon or Salmon en Croute. Her vegetables came directly out of Grampe's Garden. Stewed tomatoes, fresh chili sauce, butter pickles, and raspberry jams were "put up" for the winter. And no

matter how delicious her meal was, no matter how many ooh's and ah's it elicited, she always said "I think it's too salty" or "It could have been cooked a little more." She was a perfectionist of the nth degree.

From these two amazing women, I learned the basics of cooking. And I learned what food does: it brings people together. A gathering around a table, on fancy Wedgewood or cheap Chinette, meals were about family, love and conversation.

Honestly, as I wrote yesterday afternoon, my stomach was literally growling, and I could smell Nana's Bolognese and Grandma's roast. Agh! It made me hungry. So stay tuned. I hope to have a book out by fall.

PHOTO ALBUM

A couple of minor MetroFreshvals

Catering the MetroFresh way

Betsy and Mitchell on patio

Angel and Richie

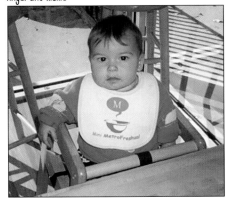

Another Mini MetroFreshval

Miss Vee selling Richie's Calendar

Greg around 2006

High powered meeting at the Wine Bar

Fay Webber — budding singer-songwriter

Poppa and Jaime

MetroFresh 1.0

Cool Chicks — Yvonne and Mara with Mitchell

Kirstin, Rockstar, Greg, Zack and Ryan

Jack Goldwasser on the Sax

Dog Park-ing

Kristin at work in 2006

MetroFresh 2.0

MetroFresh Opening Day, October 10, 2005

Halloween at MetroFresh

Opera Night at MetroFresh

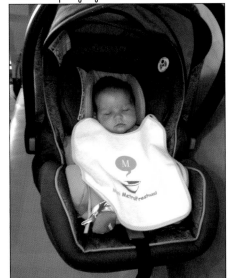

Mini Metrofreshual

PJ's Place

PJ, Dustin and Ray

Miss Vee handing out hugs

Our 1st anniversary, October 10, 2006

179

Poppa-in-a-box

Mitchell with Brendan, Tiffanie, and the kids on the patio

Our regular — Kim

MetroFresh crew around 2006

Irene, Noreen and the family

Sarah and Diane

Tiffanie and Randi

Soledad in the old kitchen

The World Cup Kitchen Crew — Viva Mexico!

Rockstar and Poppa

Mitchell with Kai McHale, 2007

Rockstar in the old kitchen

Mitchell with Victoria Price

Tio Miguel at the stove

Mitchell with Souper Jenny at Opening Night

Richie and Jeff Dauler on the patio

Richie and Madelyn Lansing

The Old MetroFresh patio

181

October 9, 2010. Anderson Family at Rumsey and Davin's Wedding

ACKNOWLEDGEMENTS

I need to first acknowledge my mentor and friend, Jennifer "Souper Jenny" Levison for giving me the opportunity of a lifetime when she made room for me in her tiny Buckhead, Atlanta kitchen. She quite literally gave me my second career. Not only did she share her knowledge, she shared her spirit and when she thought I was ready to open my own restaurant, she nudged me out the door. Jenny has been with me every step of the way. On the day I opened MetroFresh in October of 2005, she closed her shop and put a sign on the door that read, "I'm going to MetroFresh, please join me."

Creating and maintaining a restaurant for 10 years requires the dedication of so many people. It would be impossible to name all of them, however, top of the list is Bryan "Rockstar" Kraatz, my second in command in the kitchen. He's been by my side for almost a decade. His commitment to MetroFresh and the creativity of the food we serve is amazing and inspiring. We have had an ongoing conversation about food and how to create a challenging and delicious menu for our MetroFreshual family every single day. Many of the recipes in this book are a true collaboration with Rockstar.

Then there is the beautiful and efficient Sarah Peters Kraatz, Rockstar's wife, and my general manager. With her help, the wheels of the restaurant turn and without whom I never would have had the time to write this book.

Finally, in the kitchen and out front, I have the most amazing staff. My team makes MetroFresh what it is and I thank every one of them.

I'd like to acknowledge my large family for much of the material and memories on which I draw so many of my daily messages. Grandma, Grampa, Nana, Grampe, Mom, Dad, Heidi, Kris, Gerrit, Tracy, Brooks, their husbands, wives, children, and now grandchildren have influenced me in such profound and beautiful ways. From them I've learned the value of a life well lived, generosity of spirit, and how memories of the past shape our present and prepare us for the future.

Thank you to Laura Miller, my copy editor, for her patience and trained editorial eye throughout the process. Thanks to the amazing staff of Jera Publishing, especially Stephanie Anderson (no relation) for a beautiful book. Thank you to Lynne Gale for slogging through hundreds of blogs and choosing her favorites. And thanks to Lindsay Denman, who's graphic and interior design aesthetic keeps the look of MetroFresh and this book in the same visual world.

Finally, I have to thank Richie Arpino, who has accompanied me on this amazing journey for more than 18 years. Our partnership is the most important thing in my life. By teaching me to focus on the forest and not just the trees, he's helped me to accomplish so much. From leaving show business for a new career as a chef and creating a successful restaurant, to completing this book, it's always been Richie's sense of the possible, his inherent optimism and goodness that have kept me going. And, of course, having a live in photographer comes in handy when you're writing a cookbook!

The MetroFresh Family Holiday Party. 2014.